Look What the Lord Has Done

My Story

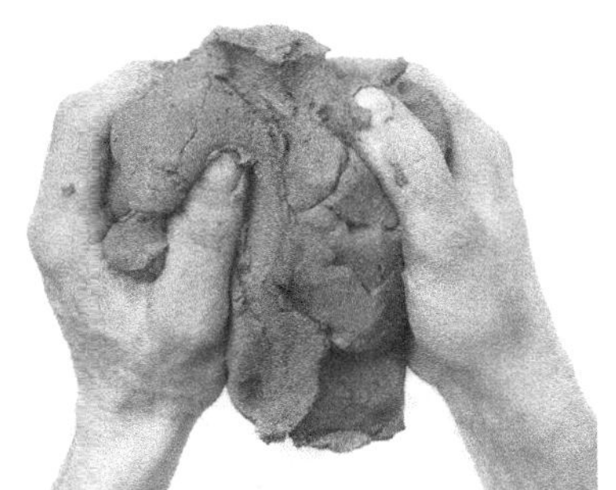

by

Ray Llarena

Look What the Lord Has Done: My Story

Published by:

McDougal Publishing
P.O. Box 3595
Hagerstown, MD 21742-3595

ISBN 978-1-58158-209-3

Printed on demand in the US, the UK and Australia
For Worldwide Distribution

Dedication

I would like to dedicate this book:

To Almighty God, the Creator of the Universe, the Giver of all life, You created me for a purpose and gave me the gift of life and, with it, all of the gifts that make me unique and individual, different from the rest of Your creation.

To the Lord Jesus Christ, who loved me unconditionally and gave His life for me on the cross of Calvary, You paid the price for my redemption so that I could be restored to the plan the Father had when He created Me after His image and likeness. Through Your death on the cross of Calvary, my life has been shaped and molded to become a vessel of Your glory and power.

To the Holy Spirit, who has empowered and enabled me to do what God has called me to do, nothing has been done by my own power. It has been by the grace You brought into my life, cultivating in me all the deposit the Father had made in my heart and in my spirit. You have mined the riches of glory, revelation, and knowledge and have deposited them in me. Through Your power, You helped me to blossom into the man I am today. From the chunk of clay, You made a vessel to give You glory and honor.

To my three precious children who are my greatest possession here on Earth, to Joy, to David, and to Leah, you are my best friends and confidantes in this life, my joy and my pride.

To the memory of my dear beloved wife, Nenita, who has now gone to be with the Lord, your memory is still alive in my heart and in my mind. You walked with me through the corridors of life and in all the pathways of service to the Lord. In the midst of obscurity, trials, and hardship, we stuck it out together with joyful heart, honoring and serving the Lord.

To every reader who has felt insignificant and of little value, like me, you may feel that you are little more than a lump of clay. This book is dedicated to you because God can transform that insignificant piece of clay into a beautiful vessel of glory and honor as you surrender your all to the Lord. May this book bring you inspiration and motivation to become the person God designed you to be.

Being confident of this very thing, that he which hath begun a good work in you will perform it until the day of Jesus Christ.
— Philippians 1:6

But we have this treasure in earthen vessels, that the excellency of the power may be of God, and not of us.
— 2 Corinthians 4:7

Prologue

Here I was pastor of a church of several thousand people in the city of Chicago, one of the largest and most exciting metropolitan centers in the world. I was having to conduct several services each Sunday in order to get everyone in, and we had a very delicate balance of getting the one group out of the parking lot and the next group in without totally disrupting downtown traffic each Sunday. I was blessed with a wonderful congregation made up of men and women of some forty-five different nationalities. In recent years, I had been taking mission trips to India, Vietnam, Cambodia, Hong Kong, Belize, Israel, etc. How had I come so far from the little Filipino barrio where I was born? Only God knows!

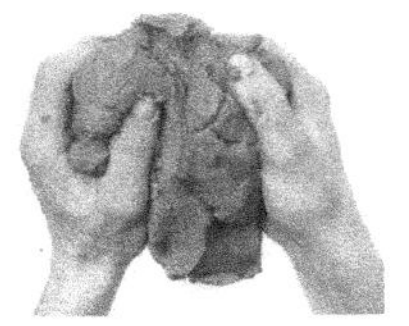

1

I HAD BEEN BORN INTO A VERY RELIGIOUS ROMAN CATHOLIC FILIPINO family, the eighth of nine children. Early each morning we were awakened by our mother to pray the Rosary, and we were taught from a very early age to honor God and to seek Him in prayer. Very young I learned how to pray the Rosary myself and to lead the family in that and other prayers. When I was just eight, I was already saying prayers for the dead.

My grandfather on my father's side was a sculptor who often fashioned idols for the Church. Before a statue was even finished, Mother would be praying the Rosary for it. We made procession with those images before they were delivered. So I grew up with a consciousness of God and fully believed that He existed.

When I was still a child, sometime between the ages of nine and eleven, I became much more involved with the Church and was even a member of the Legion of Mary. I was taught Catechism at a very young age. Although we had not yet been taught anything about the Bible, to my way of thinking, I was growing up close to God. I was sure that He was in my heart and in my mind.

The Bible was something else. Apparently it was very dangerous because we were warned to stay away from anyone carrying a book that even resembled the Bible. It was considered a sin to listen to what such people had to say or even to come close to them or their churches. I was obedient in this regard, so I grew up knowing nothing at all about the Bible.

We were in church nearly every day of the week, and it was only natural that I began to have a desire to become a priest. Early on, this became my dream. After finishing high school, I would enroll in seminary and study for the priesthood. Priests were surely very close to God, and that was what I wanted for my own life. I admired men of the cloth.

Once every three months our local priest would come to our house after mass, and we would have the privilege of entertaining him. I got acquainted with several of these priests and was sure that I wanted to be one of them — someday.

2

We were not rich, but neither were we poor. We were middle-class Filipinos. My father was a businessman and a farmer at the same time. We had a grocery store, and we also had a coconut plantation, a rice plantation, and a banana plantation. We raised our own cattle, hogs, and chickens. As I grew up, money was never a problem. I enjoyed my early childhood because we were clearly not deprived.

Our small barrio in the southern part of the island of Luzon has now grown into a city, but then it was a much smaller place. We were country people.

When I finished my elementary school, my parents went to live in Manila for a time with our grandparents, and they took me there to study. This was considered to be a great privilege. Our home place was very far from the big city, and to go to the capital to learn was something not everyone was able to do. I was twelve, and I found this new adventure to be very exciting.

For the first two years I was in Manila, things went well for me. I went to church and prayed each morning before school. Then I would stop by the church again on my way home. During those days, I learned to walk to the altar on my knees praying and to do the stations of the cross. I enjoyed doing all this because I was sure it was moving me closer to my dream of becoming a priest.

The thought of giving my life totally to the Lord brought me great anticipation. Surely the celibate life of the priests would be carefree and full of joy. Each night I prayed the Rosary with the whole family, including uncles, aunts, and cousins, and most of the time I led everyone in prayers. It was hard to see how this could all go wrong—but it did.

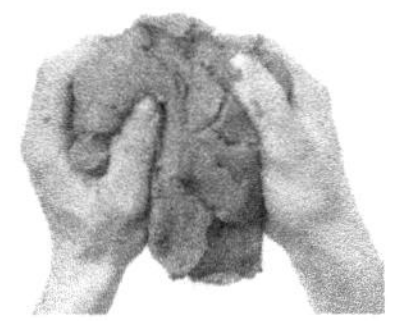

3

My parents went back to the province and left me in the care of an aunt, and I slowly began to associate with the wrong crowd. By the time I realized how this was affecting me, I was already skipping classes. This was unusual because I never skipped going to church. I was still going twice a day, going to confession every Saturday, and taking communion on Sunday. Sometimes I spent more time in the church than I did at home. But my other life was deteriorating and my schoolwork was suffering.

For one stretch of four of five months, I didn't go to class at all. I just hung out with my friends. I would leave my grandparents' home each morning with my books and return about the right time each afternoon. They and my aunt all thought I was doing well in school and never suspected what was wrong. Or, if they did, they said nothing.

Then one day a class advisor decided to find out why I had not been coming to school. She imagined that I might be terribly sick or that some tragedy had befallen my family. She went to my grandfather's house to inquire about me.

"What do you mean?" my aunt asked the advisor. "He has been going to school every day." The advisor got out my attendance record and showed it to my aunt and grandparents. It clearly indicated that I had been absent from class for the past months.

I knew nothing about this little visit, and I went home at the usual time, thinking that it would be as before. But somehow the attitude of my guardians had changed. "Where have you been?" I was asked.

"I just came from school," I assured them.

I could see that they were not accepting my story, and I knew that I was about to be severely punished.

My aunt called my mother and spoke with some of my brothers, trying to decide what should be done with me. It was decided that if I was not taking advantage of the opportunity to study in the capital I should return to the province to work on the farm. The pigs needed tending, and there were many other chores I could do. When I was told what my fate would be, I ran away rather than face my punishment.

For the next two months, I found a solitary place to sleep in one of the churches, and I stole to eat. Interestingly enough, I was still doing my daily prayers, and one day my younger brother found me there in the church.

I hadn't bathed in a very long time, and he was shocked by my appearance. He went home in tears and convinced everyone that they should feel sorry for me, and I was welcomed back into the home. But, before long, I was also sent back to the province.

4

At the time, it seemed like a terrible tragedy to me to have to leave my friends in the big city and go home to such a small country place, but God knew exactly what He was doing with my life and why I was being sent home. While I had been living in Manila, my older sister, Arsenia, had been saved and was on fire for the Lord. She and her children were living in the family home, and when I arrived there, I had to live with them. Immediately, she began to witness to me. It took her almost nine months to convince me that she was right, but through her persistence, I eventually came to the Lord. It was 1960, I was fifteen years old, and suddenly I had new life in Christ.

The desire for becoming a priest was quickly changed into a desire to become a minister of the Gospel, a pastor to bring lost sheep into the true fold. The Holy Spirit spoke to my heart and said, "You're of great value to me."

Immediately after I got saved, I received a call of God into the ministry, and fortunately, the pastor of the church where my sister was attending recognized that calling right away. He quickly took me under his wing and began to disciple me.

I was able to do meaningful things to help the pastor with the activities of the church and with the ministry outside the church. This was the beginning of a great adventure for me, and where it would end I could only imagine. Had I known that the Lord would open doors for me around the world, it surely would have been even more overwhelming. Whatever He did in the future, I sensed that it was going to be very good.

I never complain about my religious upbringing because I believe it had a lot to do with my finding God. Being zealous for God never hurt anyone. Now, however, I was able to add to that zeal a personal relationship with God.

I had been bold for what I believed all along, often arguing with Jehovah's Witnesses and other cultists, defending my faith. Now I realized how very little I had really known. Thank the Lord He found me at such a young age, and I was able to begin to learn His ways.

Growing up in a religious family also kept me from being involved in many of the vices common to the youth of our country at that time — like smoking, drinking, and gambling. As keen as I had been to spend time with my friends, I had done none of those things because of the fear of God ingrained in my heart from an early age. What a blessing! I am convinced that I did not miss anything in my youth because of it.

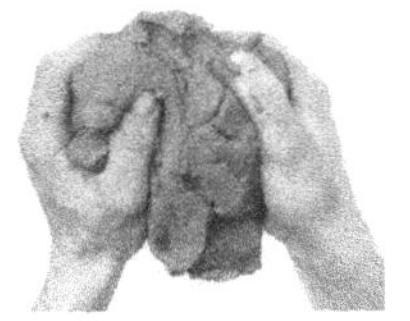

5

There was one great lack that I had felt in my early life — the love of a father. From my early childhood, I had seen very little of my earthly father. He was often sick and was in and out of hospitals. He was never around for long, and consequently I was never able to experience what it meant to be close to a father and feel a father's love. I had always felt an emptiness in this regard in my heart. There was a vacuum there. Something was missing.

When I saw other children my age walking with their fathers in the park or riding on their father's backs, I felt pangs of jealousy and said to myself, "Why is it that my father could not do that with me?" I seemed to be somehow cursed of God not to be able to enjoy this particular blessing.

It was only when I had been saved that I experienced for the first time what it was to have a loving father, and now I had the very best — Father God. Knowing that He was with me always and that His love was never-changing had a powerful impact on my life. That great emptiness was filled, the vacuum disappeared, and the relationship with my heavenly Father was far more powerful that an earthly relationship could ever have been. In the coming days, I learned the intimacy enjoyed by father and son. I learned to walk and talk with God in a very personal way.

When my sister, Arsenia, died, it was my great privilege to go home to the Philippines and conduct her funeral. It was a joy to honor her, because through her, our entire family found eternal life in Christ.

What a blessing it is to look back now and see how God's purposes and plans for our lives can be carried out — if we are just willing to answer His call. My hand was now firmly in the grip of Father God, and I knew that He would lead me into the future, protect me, and provide for my life.

Only two months after I was saved, my pastor said to me one day, "We need to find an evangelistic meeting for you to preach in." That prospect was very exciting to me, and I was sure that I was up to the task. After all, I was nearly seventeen, and I was very eager to serve the Lord.

When the day came, however, I found that I was very frightened. In fact, I was shaking with fright and sweating profusely. As I stood before the crowd, with the opportunity I had longed for, my mind suddenly went blank. The next five minutes seemed like forever. My pastor finally took over for me, and I was sure that I would never preach again. I had failed. But that pastor was wise, and he kept pushing me to try again and again, until it got easier. This was the way I got started in the ministry.

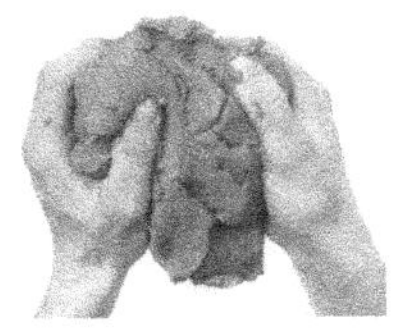

6

EVENTUALLY, I DECIDED TO GO TO BIBLE SCHOOL, AND I ENROLLED at Bethel Bible Institute, outside of Manila, an Assemblies of God Bible school. (BBI, as we all called the school then, has now become Bethel Bible College.)

I had several strikes against being accepted into the Bible school. I had not finished my high school training, I was an extremely shy person, and I had no money. I told those who interviewed me that God had called me, that I wanted to preach His Word, and that I knew I needed to be trained for the ministry. I received a qualified acceptance but was put on probation and placed in a special class. Even then, the classes were very difficult for me, and I did not get a good start to my life as a student there.

Having been extremely shy and introverted much of my life, I had never found it easy to meet people or to make friends. My natural tendency was always to withdraw within myself. This made things even more difficult now.

After I had been in the school for six months, it appeared that I would not be able to complete my studies. My teachers and other members of the faculty held a meeting to discuss what to do with me. The general consensus of the group was that they were wasting their time with me and that I was wasting my time trying to be something I wasn't cut out to be. "We might as well send him home," one of the teachers said, "because I don't think he will ever amount to anything in the ministry."

This was not the only meeting the teachers and faculty had held to discuss my future and what they should do with me. I had not been able to pay my tuition for the first six months. I also had not been able to pay my dormitory fees and my room and board. Clearly, I was not an asset to the school; I was a liability. Now, most of the teachers were in agreement. The best thing they could do was send me home. I clearly belonged on the farm.

There was one teacher for whom I have always been very thankful. Her name was Rosina Corpuz, and she has now gone on to be with the Lord. When all the other teachers at BBI had lost patience with me, Sister Corpuz took it upon herself to defend me. She turned to the other teachers, alone among seventeen of them, and said, "Who are we to decide who God can use and who He cannot use? If this young man is saying he is called of God, who are we to determine that he's not called of God?" The other teachers were momentarily startled. They had thought that everyone among them was in agreement.

Some of my "problems" were again rehearsed. "I know," she said, "but if you will give me time to work with this young man, I believe God can change him." The others were not hopeful, but they agreed to let her try.

In the coming weeks and months, Sister Corpuz helped me in many ways. Most of all, she helped me to come out of my shell.

The first thing she taught me was that I had to believe that God had a future for me. No matter how I felt inside, how things looked outside, or how others assessed my potential, I had to be sure of myself. No one else could fully understand what God had planned for me except me and God Himself.

Then she taught me that I had to start putting my faith into practice. I had to work hard at becoming what God had called me to be. "You will have to practice your reading on your own," she encouraged me. "Take your Bible, take a magazine, a newspaper, and some of your textbooks and go somewhere where no one can see you or disturb you, and begin to read aloud."

"Practice your preaching," she said. "Go to the back of the dormitories where no one will hear you. (There was a fishpond back there surrounded by trees.) Hide somewhere there and begin to practice what you will preach to others one day."

I did what she told me to do. It was interesting. I preached to the fish, and not one of them every got saved, but as I practiced, I learned how to win men.

Sister Corpuz's most important advice to me was this: "The thing that will help you the most is to develop your prayer life. If you know how to pray, God will help you in every situation." From that day forth, I didn't care what anyone else said. I was going to cry out to the Lord in prayer. I didn't really know how to pray effectively, but I did want to be closer to God, so I was determined to learn.

For the next two and a half years, God woke me every morning at three o'clock, and I would go down to the chapel to pray. If the chapel was still closed, I would kneel behind it and cry out to the Lord until five or even six. God visited me in those early morning prayer times. Sometimes I could do nothing but weep, broken before the Lord. At other times, I could feel Someone embracing me.

God made Himself real to me during those days in many other ways as well. As a young Christian, I wasn't able to understand them all, but I knew that He was there. Sometimes, when I spoke in tongues, the Lord gave me the interpretation of what I was saying, and He spoke to me of a great future.

On one of those occasions, the Lord said to me that He would take me to places where nobody would ever have dreamed I would be going. In later years, as I went into new areas, I was constantly aware that what I was experiencing was a fulfillment of what God had said to me so very long ago when I was still a student in Bible school.

That entire first year was a struggle for me academically, but I was developing a deep prayer life and a precious communion with the Lord. I was learning how to worship God (something that cannot be taught to us in a classroom or from a textbook.) I learned how to apply my faith, and slowly God began to break all of the strongholds in my life.

By my junior year, I was beginning to make great leaps of progress. God was promoting me, raising me into a new level, and even the administrators of the school took notice and began to utilize me in various ways in the school. I was given authority, I began to develop my leadership ability and to exercise right judgment about what to do and when to do it, and I sensed that my teachers trusted me. God was doing something wonderful in my life, and I gave Him all the glory.

In my second year of Bible school, I had gotten involved with a church off campus, and I eventually became the assistant pastor there. (For those who know the area, it was in Malabon, with Pastor Resus on a property donated by the Gideon Sanoy family.) In this way, I began to gain experience in how a church is to be run. At the same time, as many Bible students did, I also would go out into unreached areas to preach with the intention to start new churches where none existed. I was able to be involved in planting two such churches.

We began by just knocking on doors in a given neighborhood, with the intention of winning the family that lived there to Christ. Because of this practical experience, I was learning more than the doctrinal aspects of the faith; it was a very hands-on approach that I found very beneficial.

During our vacation times, we students would go out to various outreach churches and work the entire summer in evangelism. When these opportunities opened, I took a leave of absence from the church I was working with regularly to have this new experience and to work alongside my classmates.

Because of all of the activities, once I left the Bible school, my spiritual foundations were already strong. I graduated in 1965, and I had a consuming desire to win the lost and to build the Kingdom of God anywhere and everywhere.

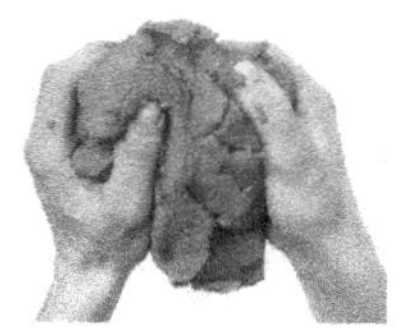

7

Once I had graduated from BBI, I sensed that it was time for me to leave my position as assistant pastor in the church where I had been working. For some time I had been praying about what the Lord's will would be for my life, and I felt that it was time for me to begin finding out.

I had long participated in one of the school prayer bands. Once a week, in our case, on a Thursday, we would gather to pray for the nations. We would divide into groups, and each group would take a certain area as a prayer burden. Just two months before graduation time, I was praying with my prayer band one morning, and when lunch time came, I felt a burden to continue praying.

Left alone in the chapel, I found a spot behind the piano, and there I cried and prayed to the Lord. "God," I prayed that day, "I don't know where You want me to go, and I don't know what You want me to do. I need direction. I want to serve You where You desire. I need some very definite direction for my life. Speak to my heart and show me Your will."

Out of nowhere, I heard a voice. I would not describe it as "audible." Rather the voice was speaking inside of me, and it said, "I'm going to make you a missionary to Guam."

That thought seemed to be so far beyond me that I found it to be frightening. "God," I said, "something like this is not what I'm asking. That would be too far out in the future for me to contemplate. I just need to know where I am to go after graduation."

I didn't even have an idea where "Guam" was. What I knew was that Guam was a foreign place, not within my own country, and that frightened me.

I got up and went to my room that day. I did not eat the rest of the day, and I kept to myself, avoiding contact with others as much as was possible. What I had heard from God had shaken me to the core.

From that day forward, when I would pray, that word would always come back to me, "I'm going to make you a missionary to Guam." That should have been a thrilling thought to someone who wanted to serve God, but it was somehow too much for me. I finally said, "Lord, I don't want to go to Guam." In the meantime, graduation day was getting closer.

During graduation week, my classmates and I were doing some serious praying. Several of us decided to form an evangelistic team and travel together for the Gospel. We would have to raise some support, but we were willing to do that. Our plan was to conduct Vacation Bible Schools around the country and use that door to win the lost. We determined to contact churches wherever we could and offer to help them. We started to the north of Manila in a small village in the mountain area called Ibatarla.

Our meetings in Ibatarla were very successful. God used us in a way that caused the churches there to be very appreciative of our efforts. When we left that town, the church had gained membership because of what we had done.

We did the same in other cities. The last city was Olongapo, the site of the largest U.S. Naval base outside of America. Because the Navy had hired large numbers of Filipino civilian workers, the city had grown considerably, and there was a great need for evangelism.

The local pastor in Olongapo housed some of us in his church, but others of us stayed in the homes of various families around town. I was privileged to be housed with a family in which the husband, newly saved, had been an officer of the U.S. Navy, but he was now retired. We had wonderful fellowship together, and he enjoyed working with us.

One day the wife said to me, "Would you be willing to go to my hometown, Santa Cruz, Zambales? It's five hours away by bus, but there is a great need there. There are no other believers. Could we do a Vacation Bible School there?"

I said," Sure, why not?"

When our time was up in Olongapo, the rest of the group left for Manila, but that man, his son, myself, and another man caught a bus for Santa Cruz. He had a house in the town, and we used that house in which to gather the children for Vacation Bible School. More than a hundred children responded.

Because there were no other believers in that place, we had expected to receive some persecution, and we were not disappointed. But we stayed for a week, teaching Vacation Bible School during the daytime and conducting evangelistic services at night. After a week, we prepared to return to Olongapo.

Again, I wasn't sure what the Lord had for me to do in His Kingdom, and I had been praying. If I didn't receive any clear direction for the future, I was considering staying on in Olongapo and working with the pastor there. On the way back to the city, my friend said to me, "It's very sad to me that we are leaving behind everything that God has done this week in Santa Cruz. I wonder what will happen to the people now. It would have been wonderful if there could have been some sort of followup to cultivate the good ground we discovered and to water the seed you have planted."

I understood what he was saying. The thought had also occurred to me. Without a church to attend, how would these new believers continue their life in Christ?

Then he turned to me again, "Would you pray about this situation?" I assured him that I would.

8

I DID PRAY, AND THE ANSWER I KEPT GETTING WAS THAT THE LORD wanted me to go back to that place, establish a church, and pastor it. It took me some weeks to become fully convinced that this was indeed the will of God for me at that moment, but eventually I could not escape that conclusion.

One of the reasons I was slow to respond to what I was feeling was that I had no financial support. One lady, when she heard what I intended to do, said that she would pay my bus fare to Santa Cruz and give me some pocket money, but that was all the security I had.

The family that owned the house in Santa Cruz had left it empty again after we had used it for Vacation Bible School, and they told me that I could use it for my own quarters (upstairs) and for the church (downstairs). That solved two more serious needs. The rest was up to God, and I was sure that He would not fail me, so I returned to Santa Cruz and began the work.

We thought we had been persecuted before, but when the local people saw that I had come back to stay and to establish a permanent church, the persecution moved into a more serious level. The local members of the Legion of Mary were determined to drive me out of that place, and they were sure that they would succeed. "The Seventh Day Adventists did not last long here," they boasted. "The Baptists were only good for six months, and the Jehovah's Witnesses also did not stay here for even a full year. You will not last long either. We're going to drive you out of this place."

But I didn't frighten easily. I was convinced that God had sent me to Santa Cruz, and I was there to stay.

The children of the village already loved me, so I had a headstart with them. I continued to gather them and teach them the Bible. We did that every night. But I also began visiting each family in the village, witnessing to them, and inviting them to come to our meetings. Little by little, with the help of the Lord, I began to win the confidence of the people.

It began with a small boy of about seven who had a hernia. A doctor had told his parents that they needed to operate on the child because the hernia was growing, but it was difficult for the child's parents to imagine how they could afford such an operation. One day they brought the child to me. They told me that they had heard people say that in some of my preaching I had declared that God was a God of miracles. "Can you heal our son?" they asked.

I said, "No, I cannot heal him, but I can guarantee you that if you will believe in God, He can heal your son. *He* is the God of the impossible." I told them I wanted the whole family to gather and hear the Gospel. They agreed to give God a chance. There were three family houses in the compound. The members of those three households gathered to hear the Gospel, and they received Christ as their Savior.

We prayed, and the boy was miraculously healed. Within a day or two the hernia had shrunk until the same doctor said that it was now "no problem." The three families now became the first serious members of the church.

One young boy of twelve or thirteen who was saved in the church was very zealous for the Lord. He often stayed with me in the house so that he could learn more about the Lord, and he also accompanied me when I visited the local people. This was serious because his mother was our leading agitator at the Legion of Mary. She would come by the house and throw rocks at it. Whenever she saw me, she would hurl verbal assaults my way. While we were having our services, she incited others to form into processions, stopping in front of our place to sing and pray (and to throw rocks). We chose to ignore all of that.

Sometimes these agitators dumped garbage into our compound, and sometimes they used human waste instead. They were sure that these tactics would intimidate me and drive me away. Then, very late one night, this woman, who was instigating all the persecution against us, sent someone to call me and ask if I would come and pray for her. She thought she was dying.

She had gotten violently ill and was in terrible pain. She had gone to a doctor, and he had prescribed medicine for her, but it didn't seem to be helping. After midnight that night, she was in so much pain that she felt sure her time had come. "Go wake the pastor," she said to one of her household members. "Ask if he will come and pray for me."

When I received this news, I was very excited. It didn't matter that it was one o'clock in the morning. I sensed that God was doing something very special. I got dressed as quickly as possible, went to the woman's house, and prayed for her. Soon after I left her that night, she fell asleep, and before long, she was well again. Although that woman did not actually get saved and become part of our church, from that day forward, the persecution in Santa Cruz stopped, and the work of the Lord grew in measurable ways.

That woman's young son was one of the first believers to be baptized in water in that place. Over the next two years, the church grew from zero to about one hundred members. God worked many more miracles for the people, and they were blessed financially until the work became self-supporting.

9

During those two years, I had many memorable experiences, and I learned a great deal from each of them. One of those experiences stands out in my memory.

Before the church began to do well financially, I went through a period when I had very little to eat, and during that time, I became very ill. I was, in fact, so ill that I, too, thought I was going to die. For many days, I was too sick to get up from the bed.

I had occasionally been known to close up the house for a few days and go to Manila to visit relatives, shop, or do other business, so even though I was upstairs in the house, no one in the town realized that I was at home.

After I had been desperately ill in my bed, unable to help myself, for a full two weeks, the Lord spoke to a friend of mine, a student at BBI, and laid it on his heart to use his spring break to pay me a visit. He boarded a bus in Manila, making the fourteen-hour trip, and came and knocked on my door.

When no one answered the door, he went to inquire of the neighbors. "He's not here," they said. "He must be in Manila. We haven't seen him for many days."

My friend wondered what he should do. He had been planning to spend the night, and it was very late to turn back to the city now. But something more serious troubled him. Somehow he felt that someone *was* in the house.

He asked the neighbors if one of their sons could climb up and look in the upper story window to make sure. They agreed to do this and were astonished to see me lying helplessly in the bed up there. They called others and were able to force their way into the house.

As everyone rushed up to my bedroom and gathered around my bed, what they saw was a pitiful sight. I had lost a lot of weight. My lips were severely cracked because of dehydration, and I had been messing myself in the bed for many days. Ants were crawling on me, they later told me.

They all gathered around and began to pray for me. I did not recover over night, but my friends were able to nurse me back to health, and I survived that terrible attack of the enemy.

Another memorable incident in that place had a similar outcome. A public school teacher from another town came to our church and was marvelously saved and filled with the Holy Ghost, and after that, she would travel by bus (a forty-five-minute-to-an-hour trip each way) to come to our services. Very quickly, she grew spiritually and became involved with the ministry.

The sister and brother-in-law of this lady, with whom she was living, became very upset with her and started persecuting her and trying to convince her to leave her new-found faith. They took her Bible and tore it to shreds. "You are well educated," they screamed at her. "Why would you become involved with something like this? We Filipinos are Catholic." To be anything other than Catholic seemed to them to be a terrible sin. Eventually, their anger turned on me as the source of their loved one's problems.

At Christmas time in December of 1966, I went to Manila to visit my family. Then I went back to my post in Santa Cruz, and we had our Christmas program. That night, after I went to bed, I had a very strong feeling that I should immediately return to Manila.

I could think of no good reason to do this, but I was restless and could not get to sleep.

I looked at my watch. It was nearly eleven o'clock, and the last bus for Manila would be leaving at midnight. Something told me that I needed to be on that bus. It was late, and I was tired and wanted to get to sleep, but eventually the restless feeling I had moved me to action. I jumped up, got dressed, packed a small bag, and left town.

Later that night, the brother-in-law of the teacher arrived at my house with his machete and a plan to kill me and rid the area of the problems caused by my teaching the Bible. He was able to climb up to the upper-story window of my house. He quietly opened it and stepped inside my bedroom. Then, sure that he was about to have his vengeance, he violently began stabbing at the bed, thinking that I was asleep there.

How long it took the man to realize that he was slashing at an empty bed I don't know, but I do know that God had mercifully spared my life once again. If I had not listened to the voice of God that night, I might have been cut into small pieces.

But maybe not. When God has a plan for our lives, and His purposes in us have not yet been fulfilled, the enemy can do what he will, and it will not prosper. God had spared my life again because I had much more to do in His Kingdom.

Another incident bears telling. As the church began to prosper in that area, the many activities were sometimes difficult for me to keep up with. Although there were many eager new believers, most of them were still so young in the Lord that I was still the janitor, the usher, the worship leader, and the preacher. Not only were we having services every night that I was in town, but

I had started Bible studies in many individual homes. I walked for long distances to reach the places where these meetings were conducted. Sometimes I had to rush to arrive home in time to get everything ready for the evening service.

One evening, I was hurrying home about six o'clock to get everything ready for the seven o'clock service, when three men jumped into my path armed with knives. "If you don't stop preaching here," one of them threatened, "we'll kill you." And they all waved their knives to emphasize the seriousness of the threat. "We'll give you a chance to pack up your things and leave town."

I said nothing, but I looked directly into their eyes, asking God to help me to be bold.

After a few moments, the man said, "One week!" He waved his knife again threateningly, and then they let me go my way.

As I continued on my way home that night, I had to calm my heart. The tension of the moment had affected me. Still, I knew that I was on a divine assignment, and I was sure that God would protect me. His presence would always be there. One thing was sure: I wasn't about to run away because someone had threatened me. I stood firm in the Lord, the week passed, and nothing happened.

Many people heard about these events, and they proved to be wonderful publicity for our ministry there. What the enemy had intended for evil God had used for good, and I was sure that He would do it again and again in the years to come.

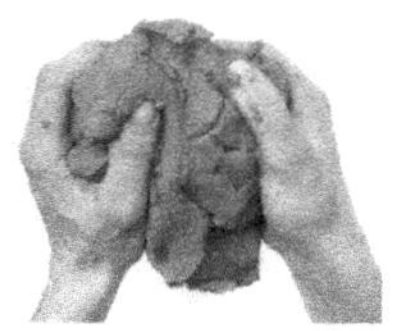

10

THE MEMBERS OF ONE NEIGHBORING FAMILY IN SANTA CRUZ, ALL saved by now, began to care for me in many wonderful ways. For instance, they began coming over to clean the church. They began calling for me to come and eat with them when it was mealtime. They began washing my clothes along with their own. The lady of the house said to me one day, "Pastor, you're busy. You don't need to cook. Just come on over when it's time to eat. You can eat with us." That was a welcome invitation, for now I didn't have to be concerned about buying food and cooking.

Another reason I loved going to that neighbor's house was to listen to Christian programming on their radio. As a pastor, I didn't often get fed spiritually, and those radio programs were important to my continued spiritual growth. One afternoon, when I was at this neighbor's house listening to a good radio program and waiting for dinner to be served, someone knocked at the door, and another divine encounter was put into motion.

We had been switching back and forth that afternoon from a news station to the Christian programming because it was also election time in our country, and Ferdinand Marcos was up for reelection as our president. The outcome of the election was of interest to us all.

The lady of the house went to the door, and I heard a man say, "Is the pastor here?" He had been to my house and someone had told him that I might be found at the neighbor's. He was welcomed in, and I was introduced to him.

"What can I do for you?" I asked.

"We heard that you heal the sick," was his answer.

"Well, not exactly," I said. I was afraid that he had confused me with the witch doctors who commonly practiced in the Philippine countryside. "I do pray for the sick, but it's the Lord who heals, not me."

"Okay, will you please come and pray for my wife?" he asked. "She has been bedridden now for fifteen years. She's paralyzed, and the only thing that moves is her neck. Her doctor has given her up to die. He said there's nothing else he can do."

He was the caretaker for some fish ponds and rice fields and oversaw the work in them. He told me where he lived, and because it was quite far and it was getting dark already, I told him that I would be willing to go with him the next morning if he wanted to come and take me to his house. The truth is that knowing that the woman had been bedridden already for fifteen years had destroyed my faith. I needed to do some serious praying.

"Come to my place at seven o'clock tomorrow morning," I told the man, who was now in tears, "and I'll go with you."

I prayed that night, secretly hoping that the man would not return in the morning. I certainly didn't want to be embarrassed or to embarrass the Lord. But, before seven the next morning, there the man was, knocking at my door, and I had to go with him.

What I saw when I arrived at this man's house was a shock. His wife was nothing but skin and bones. Her frail body was stretched out on a bamboo bed, her long hair trailing down to her waist. She looked to be near death, and I wondered what I should do.

The man must have noticed my shock because he said, "But you will pray for her, won't you?"

"Before I do anything else," I told him, "I want you to gather all of your children. I want to speak with them. Whatever else happens here this day, the most important thing is that your wife know Christ, and I want your children to know Him too."

As it turned out, some Jehovah's Witnesses had been coming to their house and holding Bible studies, so they were confused. This time of presenting them with the Gospel was very important.

When all of the family members had gathered, I preached to them the simplicity of the Gospel, and they all received Christ as their Lord and Savior. I was fully aware that many people who are desperate will do almost anything they are told, but these family members seemed to be genuinely sincere in their pursuit of Christ.

Then, that taken care of, it was time to pray for the woman. I still did not have great faith for her healing. Being paralyzed for fifteen years seemed, to me, to be a very difficult situation to overcome. I said a very short and simple prayer, asking the Lord to make His will known in the matter, and then I intended to leave.

Toward the end of my prayer, a great conviction came upon me. I could hear the Spirit saying to me, "Shame on you for not praying for this woman's healing! You're not the one who can do it. I'm the One who heals. Your responsibility is just to pray. Because you think you are the one doing the work, you are praying without faith. Pray like I'm the one doing the work, not you."

I had to ask the Lord to forgive me. Then my prayer came forth with greater zeal, and I felt something happening as I prayed. When I opened my eyes, the woman was crying. In fact, the whole family was crying, some of them with great sobs. The glory of the Lord was coming down upon them, and they continued sobbing for quite some time.

Although what we had experienced was glorious, there was no visible change in the woman's condition. I said to the husband, "If you really believe that God will heal your wife, you must take some actions of faith. For instance, your wife cannot go to church on her own, but she needs to receive the Word of God to strengthen her. If you will do your part to get her to church on Sunday, I will do my part on other days. I promise you that I will be here every morning to read the Bible to your wife while you are in the field and the older children are in school. In this way, I will continue to minister to her so that she will grow in her faith. But it is also very important for her to get to church on Sunday morning so that she can have fellowship with other believers.

"At first, it will be very difficult for her to walk and to sit. Put a cushion on a carabao sled (referring to the native water buffalo that are the beasts of burden in the Philippines) and lay her on it. Then let the carabao pull her to church." That next Sunday morning a carabao sled pulled up at the door of our church, and the lady lay there and listened to the entire service before her husband took her back home again. Then, he began bringing her every single night, rain or shine, to our services. The husband was doing his part, as he had promised.

I also did my part. For the next three months, I went to their home every day. If I couldn't make it in the morning, I went in the afternoon. Every day I read the Scriptures to that woman and taught her God's promises.

Every day, before I left her, the woman would ask if I needed anything. "Would you like some crabs?" she would say. "How about some frogs? Do you like lobster?" And her husband would bring something for me when they came to church that night. They had laying hens, and they would bring me eggs. They brought me fruit from their trees, and they also gave me money.

There were some signs of improvement in the woman's condition. Her appetite began to return, and she began to eat better. She was happy and even excited about the future, and in time, I felt that her faith for her healing was actually greater than my own. Still, when a month had gone by and I could see no dramatic change in her physical condition, it bothered me.

At that point, I began to have some serious discussions with the Lord about the matter. "Lord," I prayed, "I've been working with this woman now for over a month, and I know she's getting stronger spiritually. She's much happier than before, but still there is no sign of definite physical improvement. I need You to send us a sign to encourage our faith." A few days later, when I arrived at the home for my daily visit, I was surprised to find that all of the children were there. They had not gone to school that day, and they were very excited about something.

"Pastor Ray, Pastor Ray," they shouted as they came out to greet me. "We have a wonderful testimony to share. Our mother's feet are getting warmer."

For many years, the woman's feet and legs had been extremely cold. There was no life in them. Even in the tropical heat of the Philippines, the family had developed the habit of wrapping the cold feet and legs in cloth to warm them. This new turn of events was exciting news.

I was so encouraged by this improvement that I began going to the house twice a day, once in the morning and again in the afternoon, to encourage the members of this precious family in their faith. Every night we had been praying for the woman at the church, and every night her children had been praying for her before they all went to bed. Now, everyone was encouraged to hold on to their faith and see a complete healing.

One day, when I arrived at the house, I found all of the children so happy that they were jumping for joy. "Our mother is moving her big toe," was the big news of the day. This exciting news spread like wildfire throughout the community, and many people came to visit the woman and see the miracle for themselves. In the process, many received Christ and were healed. Our church services were more crowded than ever.

Then one day, I sent word that I would not be able to visit the home that day. I had other commitments. "I'll come tomorrow," I promised.

When I went the next day, I was greeted with more good news, this time from the husband and father of the family. "Pastor, we have a good testimony. We wanted to share it last night in the service, but we kept it because we wanted you to be the first to hear." I couldn't wait to get inside the house.

"We have a surprise for you," I was told inside.

"Yeah, well, what is it?" I asked. "Let me guess. You have another big lobster for me?"

"No, that's not it." I made a few more guesses, and they, too, were all wrong.

"Well, what is it?" I asked. "You're killing me with curiosity."

"Come on upstairs. Sit down," I was told. "Would you like some fruit? Can we fix you something to eat?"

"Thank you," I said, "but it's too early. I'm not hungry."

"Well, then," he finally said, "let's go into my wife's room," and I sensed that the mystery was about to be solved. With glowing eyes, he led me into the other room. There I found the woman sitting up and moving her legs. I began to cry for joy.

She was crying too. She said, "Pastor Ray, when I woke up yesterday morning, I was able to move." We all rejoiced together.

I explained to her husband that her muscles were atrophied from lack of use for so many years and that we needed to help her exercise so that she could fully recover the use of her body parts. He got on one side of her, I got on the other, and we picked her up enough so that she could begin taking steps. Later, she was able to hold onto some bamboo he erected for her to use for these daily exercises. For the next three or four weeks, she faithfully moved her muscles day after day, until she was able to walk on her own without any help.

On Sunday morning, Valentine's Day of 1967, this lady, having been paralyzed for fifteen years, walked all the way to the church. On the way, she passed the home of the doctor who had given her up for dead, and she stopped. He didn't recognize her (because she had gained weight and because she was walking) and asked what he could do for her.

"You don't recognize me?" the woman said.

"No, I don't," he answered. "Should I?"

When he knew who she was, he exclaimed, "My God, what happened to you? Where did you go? Who is the doctor who treated you?" She was able to tell him that she hadn't gone to another doctor but had received Jesus Christ as her Lord and Savior. "My whole family got saved," she said, "and prayer did this for me."

The doctor began to cry and said, "I believe in God, and I have always believed that He was able to perform miracles. Now I know it." This miracle was to become a testimony to the whole community.

From that time forward, the church in Santa Cruz was almost like a hospital. People came to every service seeking healing, and what God was doing gave me a great deal of prestige in the community. Many prominent citizens called on me for prayer.

When a letter arrived for me at the post office, the postmaster didn't wait for the deliveryman to bring it to me. He brought it over himself. Early in our time in Santa Cruz, it had been almost impossible to obtain a permit to hold outdoor evangelistic meetings. Now we could have permits wherever we wanted them. God had opened the hearts of the people by the demonstration of His wonder-working power.

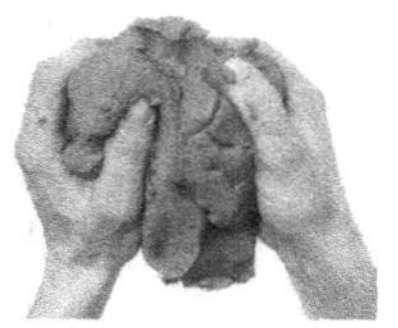

11

Right in the midst of all of this exciting activity, the Lord began to speak to my heart some things about the church in Santa Cruz that caused me to feel that maybe it would soon be time for me to move on. I had been in the town for three and a half years, and I was happy there, but why was the Lord telling me to organize the church better and to establish it and its people. I had started the church as an Assemblies of God work, so I had no real concerns about its future. It could go on without me. Now, I set in motion some programs to prepare for the day when I would no longer be there.

I decided to take a few months off and visit my family in the province. I needed some time to pray for some clearer definition of what I was feeling in my heart. A good friend agreed to take care of the church during my absence.

Passing through Manila on my way to the southern part of the island, I made a visit to Bethel Temple. At the time, this was the largest Pentecostal church in all of Asia (this happened before the emergence of Yonggi Cho's church in Korea). Bethel had been established by the late Lester Sumrall and was now being pastored by another missionary, Dan Marocco. Brother Marocco said to me, "We need help here in the big city. What are you doing way out there in the 'boonies'? Why don't you come back to the city and help us?" I could tell that he was serious.

"Well," I said, "that would be wonderful, but I would need to pray about it." I didn't tell him at the time that God had already been speaking to me about moving. What he was saying, however, seemed to be a confirmation of my feelings, and I got very excited about the prospects.

While I was visiting with my family in the Bicol region, I took time to pray. I had always wanted to be exactly where God wanted me in His harvest field, wherever that happened to be. If a new door was opening to me, I didn't want to miss it.

On my way back to Zambales, I stopped off in Manila again and visited Bethel Temple. Pastor Marocco asked me to preach. Later he said to me, "That offer still stands." I asked him to pray with me that I would know beyond a doubt the will of God in the matter. We prayed together. If I accepted this offer, it would represent a dramatic change in my life.

Something else rather dramatic was happening in my life about that time. The pastor of the church in Bicol had died, another had taken his place, and he invited me to preach on Easter Sunday morning. I had my eyes closed when they called on a young lady in the congregation to come forward and sing a special. She was singing that old favorite, Blessed Assurance, Jesus Is Mine. Oh, I love that song.

The lady's back was to me, so even if I had opened my eyes, I wouldn't have seen her face. As she sang, the Lord spoke to me very clearly: "She will be your wife."

This took me by surprise. I had not been thinking seriously about marriage or looking for a wife. I was twenty-four, but I was not in a great hurry. If this was God's will, He would have to speak to her too.

I made a point of asking about her and learned that she was Nenita Elli, also a native of the Bicol Region of the Philippines, and that she had a boyfriend, but he was not a very serious Christian. Her cousin suggested that I send her a note in which I expressed what the Lord had shown me. "I'm asking you to pray," I told her. "If this is the Lord, He will speak to you about it too." Then I spent a tense few weeks wondering what the answer would be—or if there would be an answer.

I received my answer only after a full month, but I was relieved to see that it was positive. Nenita, too, felt that this desire was from the Lord, so we began communicating seriously about our future together. We did not date even once. All of our communications were by letter.

In our culture, it was very important for our families to be in agreement, and the next step was for me to be approved by her family, so I went to the province to meet her father and made my proposal to him. He was not a Christian, and I suppose I should not have been surprised by his answer, but when you're in love, you are hoping for something different.

"No!" he said emphatically. "You just want to marry my daughter because she's a teacher, and you're looking for somebody to support you. I know your type. You should be ashamed of deceiving people to get their money so you can live without working."

Nenita said to her father, "But I love him, Daddy, and I know that this is of the Lord." But his mind was made up. He would not hear of it.

Nenita was so strong in her protest that the family ultimately decided the best thing they could do would be to spirit her out of the province and hide her with a brother in Manila. She was able to send me a note to this effect, so I knew what was happening. "They're trying to keep me away from you," the note said. "I'm going to be in Manila. Follow me."

I was able to answer that I could be found in Bethel Temple and gave the address, asking Nenita to see me there. That would be a safe place.

In the meantime, I returned to Santa Cruz, Zambales, and resigned from my pastorate there. The people were sad to see me go, but they were also happy to see that I was moving into a more influential ministry. I didn't bother them with my courting problems.

The pastor from Olongapo sent someone to pastor the church, which recently celebrated its thirty-third anniversary and is still doing well.

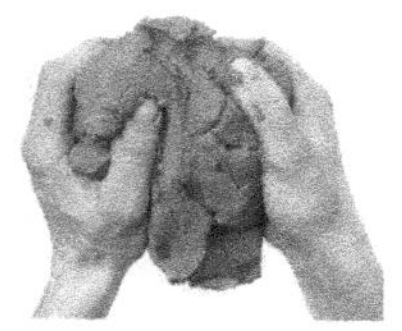

12

At Bethel, I was given several great responsibilities. I was the children's pastor, I was in charge of the bookstore, and I was the interpreter for ministers coming from abroad. This all kept me very busy.

Nenita began coming to the church, and we sometimes found a few moments alone to speak of how we could work out our future. I made sure the church leaders were fully informed about our desires, and they were praying that the Lord's will in the matter would be done.

There were no teaching positions open at that time around the capital, so Nenita was working in real estate. This required that she go out of the house once in a while, and when she did, she would call me. Sometimes she asked me to accompany her. We also spent as much time together as possible on Sunday afternoons. In this way, Nenita became more and more independent, until we felt that she could take the decision on her own for us to marry.

We were married on November 24, 1967 at Bethel Temple. No one in her family knew about the wedding until it was over. The man who walked her down the aisle was someone who was staying at the church. We were also blessed in the fact that Lester Sumrall was in town and participated in the wedding.

Nenita had left her brother's house that day, ostensibly to show property in a subdivision that was being developed. She told her family she would be away a long time because of the complications of the deal. By the time her family knew we were married it was already too late to stop us. It is not something that I recommend to young people who come to me for counsel, but it worked for us.

After Nenita and I were married, we found an apartment in Pasay City, and we enjoyed our life together, working at Bethel Temple. Two years later, our first child, Joy, was born.

In the meantime, Nenita's family was very angry with us. Her brother said that if he could find us, he would kill me. One day we were home in our apartment, and we heard a knock at the door. At first, we thought it was for the neighboring apartment. We were not expecting anyone. But when someone continued knocking louder and louder, I decided that I'd better go and see who it was. Then the person called out, and Nenita recognized the voice as her father. We looked out, and sure enough, there he stood.

Nenita was frightened. She said to me, "Don't open the door. He has a gun. It must be concealed in that basket he's carrying." But the man kept knocking, and it didn't seem right to me to leave him standing outside there. I was sure he would want to see his grandchild. Eventually we opened the door, but when we did, I grabbed the basket to keep him from shooting us. We were surprised to find that all was forgiven.

My father-in-law had been looking for us, and one of Nenita's cousins knew where we lived. There was no gun, just some gifts for the family. Over the years many members of the family were to be saved, and there are now many pastors in that family. God is so good!

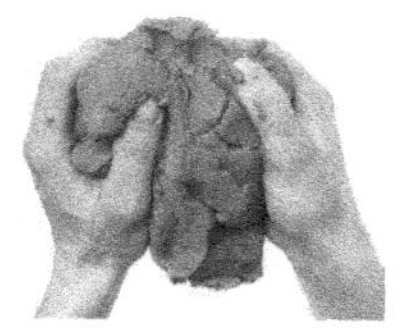

13

Joy's birth was another great testimony. Allow me to backtrack a little and tell that story. Not long after Nenita and I were married, Pastor and Mrs. Juan Soriano, who had an orphanage in Baguio, passed by the church one day. They told us that they were short of help and wondered if they might be able to "borrow" us for a while to serve as their assistant directors. We found the idea very appealing and prayed that Pastor Marocco would agree. Thankfully, he did. He felt that I had established the children's ministry at Bethel to the point that someone else could take over for the next six months. So, with his blessing, Nenita and I moved to Baguio.

We liked Baguio a lot and could not have chosen a better place to begin our married life together. The weather was cooler, the mountain scenery was very beautiful, and the people were eager to serve the Lord. We prayed that we might stay in Baguio even longer than planned.

We started a Bible school at Pastor Soriano's place and taught there, enjoying it immensely, and I also traveled to many other parts of Mountain Province, preaching and teaching in tribal villages. On these trips, I would find new students for the Bible school, and we also worked to help get churches built in those tribal regions. It was a wonderful period in our lives, and getting more wonderful all the time, and we ended up staying in Baguio longer than we had planned, until November of 1968.

While living in that lovely city, Nenita suffered two miscarriages. After the second miscarriage her doctor told her that she would not be able to bear children. We were crushed by this news. I comforted Nenita. "Well, Honey, maybe this is God's will for us so that we will not be hindered in our ministry, and we can travel freely for the Lord." But my heart was not satisfied.

Then one night I was reading the book of Samuel about how Hannah had cried before the Lord and He had given her a son. I said to the Lord, "It's not fair that You answered Hannah's prayer and You will not answer ours. You know our desire. If You cannot give us a child, then You need to erase from Your Word the promise that You are 'no respecter of persons.' Those words should not be there because You seem to favor some and not others." I had not prayed in those tones before, and I have seldom done it since, but that night I was just telling God what I felt. He seemed to be very far away at the moment.

When I got home from teaching my class one day in May of 1968, I found Nenita in bed sick. She had been too sick to cook, and the housecleaning had not been done either. She told me she felt weak and dizzy and had been throwing up all day. I said, "Well, it's probably the flu. There's a lot of it going around right now. Just stay in bed. I'll get myself something to eat."

But Nenita continued to throw up for the next three weeks and was unable to keep any solid food down. This was a mystery. She didn't seem to have any temperature, although she sometimes did feel chilled. In general, she just felt terrible.

This went on until one of our neighbors became concerned and suggested that Nenita see a doctor. She imagined that some antibiotic could clear up her problem right away. I had been giving

Nenita aspirin, but that was all we had in the house. Although the fees charged by the doctors in those days were very small, we had no medical coverage, and going to a doctor was a big step for us.

I took Nenita to a lady doctor, Dr. Yabot. She examined her and said, "We'll not give her any medication. Just give her lots of fluids — juices and water especially." But there was something else she wanted me to do: find a male and a female of a certain kind of frog out in the field and bring them to her.

"Wait a minute," I said, startled by what she was saying. "What's the relationship between a frog and my wife's sickness?"

"Trust me," she said. "When you find the frogs, bring your wife back and bring the frogs, too. Then, we'll know."

I called for some of the Bible school students and asked them to go with me to the fields to hunt frogs. We found the frogs we needed, and then I took Nenita back to the doctor's office, frogs in tow. The doctor took Nenita inside again and did some more tests. When she came out, she said to me, "Come back in one week."

In the meantime, Nenita was still vomiting, her appetite was not good, and she constantly felt dizzy. I said to her, "I'm very disturbed by what this doctor is doing. Maybe we should try to find a better doctor." I couldn't imagine what possible connection a frog could have with Nenita's suffering.

I was busy, and we didn't find another doctor, so we went back to Dr. Yabot after a week. She had Nenita in her examination room for more than an hour this time, and when she came out, she said, "Well, Reverend, congratulations."

This mystified me even more. Nenita was sick, and the doctor was congratulating me. That seemed insane to me. Seeing my consternation, she said, "Your wife is not sick. You are going to be a father."

What a thrill that news was! We still had the documentation stating that Nenita could never have another baby, but God had seen our hearts and made a very different ruling in the heavenlies.

I never did understand what the doctor did with the frogs, but somehow what she saw there told her that the results of the "pregnancy test" were positive. We were expecting again. God is so good!

Five times over the next nine months, however, Nenita nearly lost the baby. She seemed to bleed nearly as much during the pregnancy as she normally did during her menstrual cycles. At five months, she began to dilate and had to be rushed to the hospital. After she survived that scare, we decided that we should get back to Manila closer to hospitals and specialists. We contacted Pastor Marocco, and he welcomed us back.

By the time we arrived there, Nenita still had two months to go. She took life easy, while I again assumed the direction of the children's church ministry at Bethel Temple and worked in the bookstore. About that same time, Rev. David Shebley, a missionary who was heading up the T.L. Osborn Foundation support for national pioneering pastors in our country, approached me and asked if I could help him in preparing the many reports he was required to file each month. He was willing to pay us something to do that. This was a blessing because we needed the extra money. Nenita's delicate pregnancy continued to require medical attention.

Eventually, Joy was born, and we named her for what we were feeling at the moment, for she brought much joy to our lives.

Gradually, we settled back into our busy life at Bethel Temple.

14

MANY YEARS HAD NOW PASSED SINCE THE LORD HAD SPOKEN TO ME behind the piano bench at Bethel Bible Institute and told me He would one day make me a missionary to Guam. This vision would now come into clearer focus.

A Filipino man who was working in Guam began to attend the services at Bethel Temple with his wife. She was a regular member, and he lived and worked for months at a time in Guam and only came with her when he was home. When they invited me to have dinner with them one day, I received my initial information about what and where Guam was.

This man told me that the Filipino population in Guam was quite large. Many contract workers had gone there to work with the American military bases. "And," he said, "we need someone to come there and pastor those people." When he said that, it seemed almost like a knife wound to my heart, for in that moment, God reminded me of His word to me many years before.

I suddenly went numb. "God, what are you trying to tell me?" I prayed. We have settled back into life here at Bethel Temple, and now You have us going in circles again."

Before we parted that day, the man said to me, "You've got to come. We need somebody," and a dream that had laid dormant in my heart for many years began to awaken.

"Now is the time," the Lord said to me, and when He said that, I panicked. The people of Bethel Temple were taking care of us wonderfully. We had a good salary and a very nice house to live in. We had never experienced such financial security.

And the scope of our ministry was growing as well. I had been given the freedom to go out every three months and have an evangelistic crusade on my own somewhere outside of Manila. Our life at Bethel was such a wonderful arrangement that I was sure this new thought must be from the devil.

But it wasn't, and God reminded me that years before He had spoken to my heart that he would make me a missionary to Guam. I had not shared it with anyone until then, not even with Nenita. Did we want our lives to be turned upside down right now?

Things did not evolve as quickly as I had feared. As we had parted, the brother had said, "When I get back to Guam, I'm going to tell the people there that I know of a pastor who is available and have them pray for you to come." But his contract was not renewed, and his return to Guam was delayed again and again.

During Christmas of 1969 another Filipino couple (who were now American citizens) came home from Guam. They had been members of Bethel Temple previously, and now they came back to visit. They had a house near the airport and were very eager to have a Bible study started there as a prelude to establishing a church. They invited me to conduct that Bible study, and I began going there once a week.

During our times together, they talked a lot about Guam. "You need to come to Guam," they said. "We'll help you find a way to come, and you can stay with us." But then they, too, were delayed in leaving. First, it was because they were remodeling the house. Then they had problems with a daughter who was staying in the house. Then it was something else. It would be some two years before they went back. All the while, the burden continued to grow inside of me.

The whole thing didn't make sense, and I had continued to pray about it. Each time I did, the Lord had said to me, "Now is the time. Get ready." Still, I had told no one. Now, the Lord told me to share it with Nenita so that the two of us could pray together about how we were to accomplish it.

It seemed very strange to feel such an urgency and not be able to share it with the Maroccos. I couldn't understand why the Lord didn't release me to do that. In fact, I determined on several occasions to tell them everything. It just seemed the right thing to do. But every time I tried to tell them, the Lord stopped me and would not allow me to do it. The words would dry up in my mouth, and I could not utter them. I was becoming more and more restless and knew that I absolutely had to do something. But what?

I had met another American missionary couple working in our country, Harold and Diane McDougal. We probably first met when they came by the Bethel Temple offices to borrow films to use in their evangelistic outreaches. They had invited me to speak at one of their churches near Camp Murphy in Quezon City, some of their team had come to speak at Bethel Temple, and more recently we had worked together on the Morris Cerullo crusade. The relationship had slowly developed, but it was still little more than a casual one. God, however, had a plan to use them to help us.

By 1970, there were times when I wasn't sleeping well. The Cerullo Crusade and its many associated events was a welcome distraction. We invited pastors from all across our country, and we arranged for transportation and housing for them. There were many other details to be arranged as well. But once the crusade was finished, I said to myself, "What will I do now?"

I had been feeling so strongly about Guam that I even wondered if I might be called away to serve there before the crusade actually took place. Brother Cerullo needed good interpreters, but I was willing to assign this responsibility to others if I had to go before the time he needed my help.

One Sunday afternoon, I was invited to speak in the Murphy church when Sister Ruth Heflin and her brother, Wallace, were there. I was led to speak on the crossing of the Red Sea, and Sister Heflin prophesied over me that day. The word she gave was that God was going to open the way for me. It was a powerful word that confirmed to me that God was about to do a miracle on our behalf.

On a later occasion, I was again invited to preach in Murphy, and Brother McDougal asked me to come a little early and have dinner with them. While we were waiting for others to come, he asked me what my plans were for the future, and for the first time, I felt led to share my burden for Guam with someone outside of our family.

He didn't say much. He listened, and then he prayed that God would have His way. He shared with me two things: how he and his wife had come to the Philippines when she was expecting and they had very little financial guarantee from anyone except the Lord, and how God had been speaking to him recently about Filipinos going out as missionaries to the nations. Nothing more was said of Guam that day.

As the time for the Cerullo crusade arrived, I was less involved. His team had found an interpreter they felt could do the job, and all the preliminary arrangements that had taken us so many months to accomplish were all finished. Then someone called to say that they were not entirely happy with the arrangements for interpreters, and they wanted me to help.

The first night of the Cerullo meeting was powerful. Brother Cerullo's message built up my faith. It seemed that God had sent him just for me. Interpreting for him that night became a double blessing. I was able to voice the message to the people in our native Tagalog, but at the same time I knew the message was for me, and I was receiving it. I got very excited.

Not long after the crusade Harold McDougal called me again and asked me to come and speak with him on the matter of Guam. He said that they had been praying about what I told them, and that he believed God was going to make a way for me to go. If God was calling Filipinos to become missionaries to the nations, then I should be the first and set the example for others to follow. He asked me to make some inquiries about what was needed as far as paper work. He encouraged me to begin getting the papers I could, to make an airline reservation, or to take any other steps of faith I could. If I did what I could by faith, then God would do the rest, he said.

I called a travel agent and made flight reservations to Guam and I inquired about the needed paperwork. As it turns out, this was to be a major hurdle. Because Guam is a protectorate of the United States, securing a visa to Guam was just as difficult as getting a visa to the United States. In fact, it was the very same process.

I would need a letter of invitation from Guam or papers from an American organization sending me to Guam as their representative. I relayed all of this information to Brother Harold.

It took time for all of these papers to be processed. Harold had to find a willing heart in his organization in Maryland, someone willing to stick his neck out for someone he didn't even know. And then there was the waiting, and waiting, and more waiting. At one point, we were told that our papers had been lost, and they were not found until seven weeks later.

Finally, in the summer of 1971, everything was approved. When it all fell into place, I was amazed. God had brought me from obscurity and rejection, had given me some years to taste the hardships of the ministry and had shown me how to persevere. He had brought me to Manila to make all the right contacts, and now He was launching me out to the nations. How grateful I was! And how humbled!

In late December of 1971, we finally boarded a plane for Guam. It was seven years, almost to the day, that God had spoken to me about becoming a missionary to that land. It had taken a great miracle!

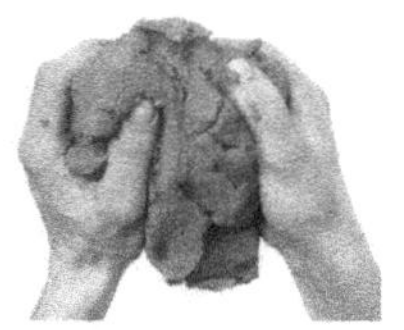

15

DURING THE TIME WE WERE WAITING FOR OUR PAPERS TO BE PROCESSED, I prayed about going to AOG church headquarters and telling the national leaders about what God had planted in my heart. I felt that they might support us in this venture, at the very least sending us to Guam. I requested an appointment, and a date was set.

On the assigned day, I sat before my brothers and carefully relayed to them the entire sequence of events that had brought us to this point. When I had finished, they all looked at me for a while without saying a word. Then one of the pastors spoke up.

"We don't have a mission program for Filipinos,"he said.

Another officer said, "Young man, it's good to dream, but you're dreaming the impossible dream."

They were not able to encourage me in any way. If they had only dared to say, "If this is of God, He will bring it to pass," I would not have left their presence nearly as discouraged as I did that day. But God is not limited by our small thinking, and He was about to move upon the people who could help us bring our dream to pass.

When our papers were approved and the visas were issued, only then did I feel free to tell the Maroccos what I was planning to do. We still had no ticket and no money, but I knew that the time to depart was getting closer. The Maroccos were not very happy with our announcement. They had been good to us, and they hated to lose our help at Bethel Temple. They were not led to encourage us in any other way.

I called Brother McDougal to say that the visa had finally been issued and to thank him for all that he had done to make it possible. "Wonderful," he said, "when are you leaving?" Well, I still wasn't sure. Only God knew.

We were led to reserve seats for Guam, but those seats were hard to come by, and the travel agent was reluctant to reserve a seat for us before having the cash in hand. He made a suggestion that sounded very good to us. He told us that Pan Am had a program in which contract workers could fly now and pay later from their future earnings. Maybe we could use this same program.

He went on to say how plentiful jobs were in Guam and that it would be easy for Nenita and me both to find good-paying part-time jobs once we got there and then to pay off the airfare over time with easy installments. He took us in his car to the office of Pan American Airways, talking enthusiastically all the way.

Nenita and I were initially very excited about this prospect, but when we got to the Pan Am office and were climbing the stairs to the particular office that handles these matters, suddenly the Spirit of the Lord arrested me. I could not take another step. The Lord spoke to my heart and said, "If you do this, before you even leave your country, you will already be in bondage. You will be bound, not free. You will go out being a slave. How can you go like this and still do the ministry I am sending you to perform? I'm not sending you there to work and pay off airline tickets. I'm sending you to work for My Kingdom."

A sudden fear came upon me, and I realized that this was not what we wanted. "Let's go," I said to the travel agent who had brought us.

"Why?" he said. When I tried to explain to him, he said, "At least fill out the application. That doesn't hurt anything. Then you can take your time and think it over. But if you do decide to take advantage of it, your paperwork will be here."

"No!" I answered. "I just feel that the Lord doesn't want me to do this."

He very kindly dropped us off at the church, and I went into the prayer room to call on God. I was crying, not understanding what was happening to us.

I wasn't in the prayer room very long before someone came to call me and say that I had a telephone call. It was Brother McDougal. "So, when are you leaving?" he asked.

"I don't know," I said, hoping that my sniffles could not be heard across the phone line. "We have no ticket yet. The agent did give us a temporary reservation, but we have only seventy-two hours in which to redeem it, or it will be relinquished." He didn't say much. He did say that they would keep on praying and believing for us.

We lost that reserved space, and the following week I was praying again. It was getting closer to Christmas, and for some reason, I felt that we should celebrate Christmas in Guam. We needed to leave the Philippines before Christmas. Two days later Brother McDougal called back and said, "Congratulations, you're leaving for Guam."

I said, "No, I don't yet have any ticket."

"You do now," he said. He explained that he had gotten some money together (I was later told that many of his students sacrificed to make it possible). It had been impossible to find any seats in economy class before Christmas, so they had made first-class reservations for us, he was telling me. "Diane is in the Philamlife

Building (downtown, not far from me) right now. Can you meet her there?"

Could I? I ran the blocks to the Philamlife Building, and there Diane and I were dancing together, rejoicing in the miracle God had done. People around us might have thought we were crazy, but I had never felt more sane in my entire life.

Later, as I made my way back to the church, I was weeping, but they were tears of joy, to a God who knows how to bring impossible dreams to reality.

Several days before Christmas, we finally boarded a PanAm flight for Guam, and we rode in the first-class compartment. It was an amazing prelude to the greatest trial we had ever yet experienced.

16

I had learned through the years how very important it was to know the will of God and to obey Him, but I had also learned that this was not always an easy thing to do. God hasn't promised us a bed of roses. When we are doing the right thing, there will always be opposition, and often God tests us to see what we are made of. If we can be strong through these tests, great things lie in store for us. So when things are going well, it doesn't mean that we are in the will of God, and when things seem to be going against us, it doesn't mean we are out of His will. As we entered the challenge of missionary life, we were about to be tested in a very new way.

We arrived in Guam, very excited, and sensing that we were launching into something new and wonderful, sure that we were in the perfect will of the Lord. If we had anticipated what lay ahead of us, we might have been slow to embrace it. Thank God that we had no idea of what was about to take place.

God is merciful and gracious, and He knows our limitations. Consequently, He rarely shows us the whole picture. It would frighten us too much. He takes us one step at a time. If this were not so, if He showed us immediately all that we would encounter and experience, few would be able to follow the will of God.

We arrived in Guam, not knowing anyone there. Some of the Filipinos we had met who worked in Guam were not able to return until a few years later. The first man I had met, the one who was so anxious for us to pastor in Guam, actually never returned to Guam again.

As we had been about to leave for Guam, a lady in the church had told us that her husband was working there and asked us to look him up. The children of another family said to us, "Our parents are there. Please look them up." Those were the only contacts we had.

We arrived in Guam with $64.00 in our pockets and the belongings we had in the four pieces of checked luggage the airline allowed us (the weight allowance was much smaller in those days, so these were not large pieces of luggage). There we were, the three of us (Joy was eighteen months old by this time), with no place to go and no guarantee of support coming in.

Some might wonder if we were naive or crazy or both, but we were just foolish enough to believe in the will and purpose of God. He had called us, and He would take care of us — somehow. As I look back on those experiences, I thank the Lord for allowing us to go through them. And I would not be reluctant to do it all over again if God would ask me to because in it I discovered the great grace of God.

Before leaving our country, the Lord had been imprinting in my heart the truth that He would never guide us and then not provide for us. I was sure that He knew what He was doing, and all we had to do was follow Him.

But now that we were actually there, alone and with so little, things suddenly looked much more difficult to me. We could not check into a hotel because the going rate was $60.00 a night, and we didn't have even enough for one night. What should we do?

Without us knowing it, one of the ladies of the church had called her mother on Guam and told her that we were arriving and given her the time. This lady was there at the airport to meet us. As we were gathering all of our belongings, she said to us, "You're welcome to stay with us, but don't be shocked by our quarters. The place where we are living is in the 'boonies,' and it is nothing very desirable. But there is an extra room there, which you can use." Her husband was waiting outside with his car, and they took us to their home.

We spent a few nights with them and then they took us to see a house that was, they said, "very reasonable." It was an old building far from the freeway. Of the seven posts that supported the crude native structure, three were not even touching the ground. This made the building lean precariously.

There were six steps leading up to the house, and the second one was broken. Someone had set a cookie can under one edge of it to support it. The step moved ominously when we tried to use it to go up to the house.

There were only two dangling light bulbs in the house, one in the kitchen and the other in the bedroom. These were fed by an extension cord connected to the landlord's house. Other neighbors seemed to have the same arrangement, and other extension cords could be seen as well.

They led us to the room they were suggesting as a bedroom. It had not been used for a very long time. I could see daylight through the roof, and everything was covered with a thick carpet of dust. The only thing in the room seemed to be piles of old newspapers. Those newspapers came in handy. We used newspapers as our broom to sweep the place out the best we could. Then we used newspapers as the foundation for our bed that first night. Another extension cord was connected for a light in that room, and we were in our new "home."

The mosquitoes on Guam were big, and they were active. After we turned out the lights, we could hear them buzzing about and dive bombing to attack us quickly and steadily. When they bit and sucked blood from us, it was very painful. Nenita and Joy were having difficulty sleeping.

I finally dozed off, but I was awakened suddenly about one-thirty or two in the morning at the sound of Nenita crying. She was sobbing loudly. At first, I thought she must be praying.

"Is everything okay?" I asked.

"Yeah," she answered, "just leave me alone." The tone of her voice made me know that she was definitely not praying and that there *was* something wrong.

"What's wrong, Honey?" I asked.

With that, she blurted out what was troubling her: "Is this what you kept telling me was 'the will of God'? I grew up poor, but I never had to sleep in these kinds of conditions. Look at your daughter. She can't even sleep. Look at these mosquito bites on her."

She was quiet for a moment, and I was hoping that she had gotten it all out and would be better in the morning, but she was not nearly finished. "I'm going home tomorrow," she continued. "I'm going back to Daddy. I can't take this 'missionary' life."

I still wasn't taking her very seriously, and I said to myself, *Go ahead and try. We came here on a one-way ticket, so you have no return ticket.*

But Nenita wasn't kidding and she wasn't finished. "I think it was just you who wanted to come here. This was never 'the will of God.' God would never have allowed this to happen to us after the way we have followed and obeyed Him. This shouldn't be."

She went on this way, venting her anger on me, for the best part of forty-five minutes or an hour. But I knew she wasn't really angry with me; she was angry with God.

I said, "Honey, being angry like this won't help anything. Why don't we just pray and worship the Lord."

She said, "You pray by yourself. You worship the Lord, but leave me alone."

Now I was losing my patience. "You are becoming silly," I said, "acting like a little child. God is not going to help us if you have this kind of attitude."

She did not respond. She was pouting, and I could tell that she was still very angry.

Suddenly, what Nenita had been saying for the past hour was beginning to affect me. "She's right," the enemy was saying to me. "Look what has happened. You left a very good life, thinking you were doing the right thing, and now what do you have? Is God punishing you for something? Why would He let this happen to you? You'd better go back or your family will suffer even more."

I wish I could say that I stopped this nonsense there, but I allowed it to continue for a while. "This is amazing," the enemy said. "You left a poor country, thinking that you would be better off over here, and now look at you. You're miserable."

In the end, I knew only one thing to do. I didn't have all the answers, and I didn't understand what was happening to us, but I knew God. I began to cry out to Him for mercy. As I did, He reminded me of the words of the apostle Paul: *"I have learned, in whatsoever state I am, therewith to be content"* (Philippians 4:11). In that moment, the Spirit of the Lord spoke to my heart and said, "If you will be happy and thankful and will rejoice in Me in spite of your condition, I will bless and prosper you. If you will continue in this attitude, I will shut the windows of Heaven and you will become miserable and barren for the rest of your life."

It was so powerful that I immediately began to worship the Lord, to thank God for His goodness. Before long, the glory of God came down upon me, and His sweet presence could be felt in that filthy place.

I sat there for quite a while, rejoicing in God's goodness, remembering all of the favor of past years and thanking Him that He has never changed and never would. Then, suddenly, Nenita was sitting beside me, and we were worshiping together. Her hands were lifted up before the Lord, and she was also declaring His goodness.

Then we were holding each other and crying and praising God together. We were repenting of our murmuring and complaining and asking each other and God for forgiveness. We stayed that way for a long time, so happy together in God's presence. We knew in that moment that whatever came, we were ready for it.

Our hearts were settled. We knew we were in the will of God, and we knew that He would take care of us. If He could provide for the children of Israel in the wilderness, He could provide all of our needs as well.

By now it was nearly four in the morning. I told Nenita to lie down, and I kept watch, driving away the mosquitoes from her and Joy so that they could sleep for the next few hours.

Early the next morning, Nenita was concerned about going out to find something for us to eat, and she needed milk for the baby. We didn't know which direction to start walking, so we just set out. After about a mile, we found a store where we could buy a few things.

That $64.00 would have to go a very long way. That first morning we bought a writing pad, some envelopes, and a pen for writing letters, some milk, a few drinking glasses and something to fix for breakfast that morning. Then we walked back home and had our breakfast. After we finished breakfast, we sat looking at one another, wondering what to do next. What did the future hold for us on this island?

After we were in Guam for a few days, the lady who had received us at the airport and loaned us the room told us that she had decided to return to the Philippines, and her husband would be going back to stay in the company camp with the other men. We could have the use of the whole house if we wanted. We declined this offer but did ask if we could use their house as our official address for the time being. They agreed.

The rent on the house where we were staying was only two dollars a month, so now, we had a house — such as it was, but our only contact on the island had left, and we were alone. No one knew that we had very little money left, no one but God, that is. We met a few people from time to time, when we went out to do evangelism, and they all supposed that we were well supported. We didn't tell them any different.

Gradually, we explored more of our new "house." The only toilet was down the steps and outside. It was a pit with a concrete slab over it. There was a crude low wall around the toilet, but it was not very sturdy, and there was no door and no roof to it. At night, we had to use a flashlight to find our way down the steps and around to the toilet.

One wonderful feature of our new "home" was that there were many fruit trees on the property behind it, and the owner told us to feel free to eat the fruit from them. There were papayas, pineapples and coconuts. One thing was certain, although we might have to climb a coconut tree to get its fruit, we would not starve.

17

WE HAD NOT BEEN IN GUAM LONG BEFORE WE MET THE LOCAL PASTOR of the Assemblies of God church. The lady of the house had told us that there was a church about four or five miles away. She had not been able to attend regularly because her husband (who was not a believer) used the car for his work, and she had no transportation. "See if you can find out what their telephone number is," I encouraged her. "We'll call them and find out how we can meet."

After she had secured the phone number for us, we walked to the store to use a telephone. I called the pastor and introduced myself to him, telling him that we were ministers from the Philippines and that we would like to attend his church. I also inquired about any Christmas activities they would be having. He seemed like a very fine brother.

"How can we meet?" I asked.

"Well, where are you now?" he asked.

I told him about the store I was calling from.

"Oh, I'm not far from there," he said. "If you can stay there for a few minutes, I'll come there and see you." He came, and we had a little time of fellowship. As we were parting, the pastor said, "Give me your phone number."

"We don't have a telephone yet," I told him. What an understatement!

"Well," he said, "if you'll give us a call, we'll have someone come by for you to bring you to our services."

It wasn't necessary the first time. The woman we were living with convinced her husband to drive us all to church for the

Christmas services. Before we left the church that day, the pastor said to us, "Give us your address, and we'll have someone pick you up for Sunday services. Apparently the house where we were staying had no street address, but the man who had brought us described to the pastor how to get there.

On Sunday morning, we got dressed early and then we walked to the nearest intersection to meet our ride. We were embarrassed to think that anyone, let alone the pastor, would see the conditions we were living in. He came personally for us. When he saw where we were standing, he said, "Why did you wait here for me? I could have picked you up at your house." We answered something about needing to walk and wanting to see the countryside.

That morning we were introduced to the congregation. I was asked to give a word of greeting to the people and to explain why we were in Guam. We enjoyed the service.

The man who led the worship in the church that morning was a chief in the U.S. Navy, Joseph Broussard, and he sat next to us during the service. Afterward, he asked to speak to me privately. When we were out of earshot of others, he slipped a crisp twenty-dollar bill into my hand. "Here," he said, "the Lord spoke to me to give this to you. I would like to meet with you sometime this week if possible because I want you to come and teach at my Bible study inside the base."

I said, "Okay, let me know when you want me to come."

The pastor had a board meeting after the service, so he asked one of the ladies of the church, a Mrs. Tillman, if she and her husband would take us home. They lived in the same direction. Mrs. Tillman, it turned out, was president of the women's ministry of the church. As we got close to the place where we were living, my wife said to Mr. Tillman, "Just drop us off at the corner, and we can walk from there."

"That's silly," he replied. "You're already in the car. Why walk, when we can take you? It will be faster." He was driving, so there was nothing we could say.

Nenita leaned over to me and whispered, "Don't invite them upstairs." Her fear was not only for them to see the squalor in which we were living. They were big people, and she wondered if the house might collapse under the weight of all of us.

But my Filipino upbringing would not allow me to be silent. I had to invite them in: "Would you like to come up?" I said, holding my breath, wondering if they might take me up on the offer.

"No," Mrs. Tillman answered. "We need to hurry back home because my husband has to report for duty." We were relieved.

As they dropped us off, Mrs. Tillman said, "Would you like to go to church tonight? I'm going, and I could come by for you."

"Sure," we answered. "We would love to go."

She picked us up that evening, and we went to church with her, and afterward she dropped us off again. We went to bed that night very happy. We had found a good church, and we had more than twenty dollars in our pockets.

"God is faithful!" I told Nenita. "He will never abandon us!" And we went to sleep with thanksgiving in our hearts.

Before we slept, however, we had to laugh together, thinking what it would be like for our family members and friends to see where we were at that moment and how we were living.

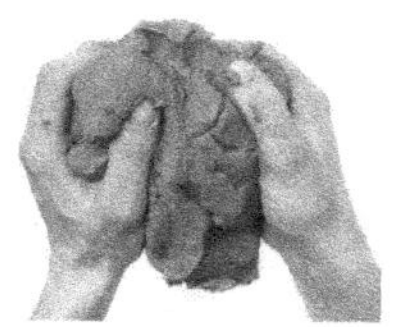

18

WE WOKE UP EARLY THE NEXT MORNING AND WERE TALKING ABOUT the goodness of the Lord again, when suddenly we heard a car that seemed to be coming our way. We jumped up and looked out the window. "Oh, it's Mrs. Tillman," I said.

"Get down there," Nenita said, "I don't want her to come up here. It's embarrassing." And it was embarrassing. We didn't have a table or chairs, and we were eating sitting on the floor.

I went down the steps quickly and Nenita followed me. "Good morning," I greeted Mrs. Tillman. "Is there anything we can do for you."

She got out and gave each of us a hug, and then she burst into tears. "I hope you will not be offended by what I want to do for you," she said.

I said, "What do you mean?"

She opened the rear gate of her big station wagon and showed us that it was loaded with boxes and paper bags. She said, "I brought all of this for you. I hope you can use it. Some of these things are brand new, and some are only slightly used." She began to tell us what had happened.

The night before she'd had difficulty sleeping. She would close her eyes, only to see Nenita and me smiling and happy. She said to the Lord, "How can these people be so happy living in those terrible conditions?" She kept visualizing the house we were living in and could not understand how anyone could be so content and satisfied in such a place. I didn't mention to her that we had cried and been angry the first night and that the Lord had told us to rejoice and He would prosper us. But it all came back to me in that moment. He had been true to His word, and He was now opening the windows of Heaven for us.

Nenita was afraid for Mrs. Tillman to come into the house, so one-by-one, we took the packages and carried them upstairs ourselves. Then, quickly, Mrs. Tillman excused herself, saying that she needed to drive her husband to work. She said she would come back in the afternoon because there were some other things she wanted to bring us, especially a playpen for Joy to sleep in, and she left.

Nenita and I went upstairs and began opening the packages. We were like little children. "Look at this!" one of us would shout. "Look at this!" the other would add. There were towels, pillows, pillowcases, blankets, knives, cooking utensils, plates, and glasses. There were foods of every type, including frozen foods and expensive fruits like apples, grapes, and oranges. There were pork chops, steaks, and chicken. How would we keep it all?

There was a sewing kit, Nikes for Nenita, and clothes for Joy. Our Christmas had come a little late, but it had come. It seemed that everything we could have asked for had arrived. In the midst of looking at everything we had been given, we started crying and rejoicing in the Lord. How wonderful He is!

We didn't know where to put the food. The family that had moved out had left a small refrigerator, but what would we do with the frozen goods? It was quite warm on the island, so we wrapped the frozen things in old newspapers to protect them.

Things had just settled down a couple of hours later when we again heard a car approaching. "Oh my," I said, "she's back already. She must be bringing the playpen." But this was a different vehicle, a dark red Toyota pickup. In it was a Filipina lady. We greeted her in Tagalog.

"No," she said, "I'm a Filipina, but I don't speak the language. I was born in Hawaii of Filipino parents, but I've never been back to the Philippines."

"How did you get to Guam?" we asked.

"I'm married to a serviceman, and he's stationed here in Guam."

I said, "How did you find out about us?"

She said, "Well, Mrs. Tillman called me. I want to bless you too." Her pickup was loaded with good things.

"I know what Filipinos like," she said, "so I brought some special things," and she began unloading all of our favorite foods, especially seafoods.

After the lady had left, we tried to decide what we were going to do with everything. Again, we wrapped the frozen foods in newspaper, then we put them into paper bags and covered them all with a blanket.

Beyond that, we decided that we were going to have to feast for several days. Nenita started cooking, and we had steak for lunch and dinner that day. Oh, my! We had begun with nothing, then we had received an abundance, and now there was a superabundance.

"We need to buy a freezer," Nenita told me. But we had no money to buy a freezer and no way to haul it home if we did. All things would come in their time. That day seven ladies came with loads of things for us. Nenita joked that we had enough to open our own little grocery store.

At five that afternoon, a pickup pulled up and a tall American and his Fijian wife got out and came up to the house. They, too, had heard about us from Sister Tillman, but they didn't want to duplicate what everyone else was bringing. "What do you need?" they asked.

Nenita answered, "We have a big problem. So much wonderful food has been given to us, and we have no way to keep it. Look at all this," and she showed it to them.

The man said, "Well, we can help you. We have an empty freezer at our house that you can use. The problem with bringing it over here, though, is that your current is not strong enough. If it's okay with you, we'll just take all of this frozen food to our house and keep it for you. While we're at it, why don't you just come over to the house and have dinner with us. And, you can spend the night with us if you want to." That man and his wife became our first close friends in Guam.

We loaded all the frozen things into their pickup and took them to be placed in their freezer. Then we had dinner together and spent the night at their house. The next morning they dropped us off at home.

Later that morning Nenita said to me, "We need to do something to balance the weight in this house. Can you feel it?" I had. When we walked into the house, we could hear some new squeaks and strains. The canned goods stacked to one side were overbalancing one part of the house, and she was afraid it might collapse. We spent some time that day distributing the weight of our blessings around the house. What a good problem to have!

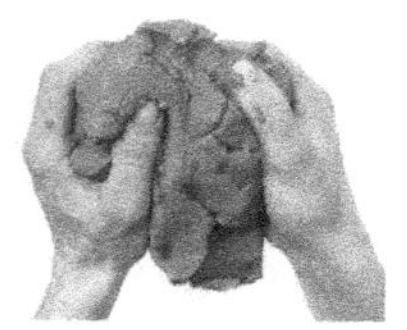

19

Joe Broussard had been trying to reach me. Learning that we had no telephone, he came to visit. Since everyone knew about our situation already, we were no longer embarrassed to invite the church people into our home.

"I'd like for you to go with me tonight and teach the Bible study," he said. "We can have dinner in the ship. Your wife can't come because it's just for men."

After the Bible study, we were on our way home when he asked me, "Are you in a hurry to go home?" I said I wasn't, and he parked the car so that we could talk for a while.

Joe began to share his heart with me. His wife and children, also good Christians, were in Waukegan, Illinois, and he sometimes got lonely. "I would love to fellowship more with you folks to give me something to occupy my mind and pass the idle hours," he said. I told him that would be wonderful.

"If you would come and teach the Bible study every week, then we could have fellowship," he said. I told him I would be glad to do that. He continued, "I'd like to share something with you that happened the first Sunday you were at church. I had gotten my pay and sent most of it to my wife and children. All I kept was twenty dollars for miscellaneous expenses. My food and lodging is free, but I do need to buy gasoline.

"While I was leading the worship that morning, the Lord spoke to me and told me, "Give your twenty dollars to that missionary."

I said, "Lord, I can't give that money. It has to last me until my next paycheck. Later, when I was sitting next to you, I had my hand in my pocket holding onto that twenty-dollar bill. But the urge to give was too strong, and I eventually had to do it." What he didn't know was how much that twenty-dollar bill had meant to us. We held onto it for a long time, not wanting to spend it and not having to spend it, because God was providing for us in so many other ways.

After Joe dropped me off at the house that day, Nenita went outside to sweep up leaves in the yard, and I was trying to fix something or other to improve our humble quarters. She came in and said jokingly, "I wish somebody would loan us a bed."

Joy now had a better place to sleep, and we all had mosquito nets that allowed us to rest undisturbed by those vicious creatures. Now, Nenita wanted a bed.

Before noon that day, the son of the lady we had met in the Philippines came (she had agreed for us to use her address for our mail, but we had not stayed at her place). We had met the young man in church and learned that he was related to the family we knew. He was coming now with a letter for us.

"Who would have sent us a letter at that address?" we wondered. We had been in Guam nearly a month by that time, and this was the first such letter we had received.

The letter was from Lloyd Baker of Hagerstown, Maryland; he was the co-worker of Harold and Diane McDougal who had helped file our papers for the visa to Guam. The letter began, "You don't know me, and I don't yet know you personally, but we had the privilege of working out your papers for the visa to Guam. I just wanted to introduce myself to you.

"I am a postman. I deliver letters, and my salary is not large. But the Lord has been impressing upon my heart to send you this check. We will be sending more sometime later." The enclosed check was for $46.35.

Now we had a twenty-dollar bill, some loose change and a check for $46.35. I wondered how we could cash the check. We hadn't yet opened a bank account in Guam because there had been no reason to do so. We asked the pastor if he could help us to cash the check, and he gladly did us that favor.

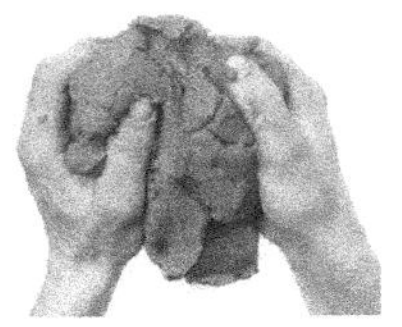

20

One day the pastor came to visit us. "I'm amazed that they accept your rent here," he said. "They should be paying you to stay in this place. I think I have a short-term solution for you. We have a neighbor, an American, who is looking for someone to watch his house while he and his wife are in the States on leave. He's not a Christian, but they are good people. It would only involve being sure to feed their dog and cat every day. I mentioned you to him, and he said he would be willing to pay you something to stay in his house for two weeks, and they would leave plenty of food for you. Would you be interested?" Then he added, "It's a beautiful house by the beach."

"Well," I said, trying to hide my intense joy, "we would be glad to stay in his house, and he wouldn't have to pay us anything." There was no more discussion. It was agreed.

In the meantime, our problem was what to do with all the groceries stored in the little house we had been living in. If the house was left empty, everything would be quickly stolen. We spoke with the family that was already keeping our frozen goods, and they agreed to also store our other items in their basement. The pastor helped us pack everything up and deliver it to the other home for storage, and then he delivered us to our new housing.

It was indeed a lovely house. It was fully air-conditioned, and it had complete appliances, including radio and television, something we had not seen in quite a while. "Wow!" Nenita said. "Now we really have it made."

The owner had left already, and there was a note on the table. "There is plenty of food in the freezer," it said. "Help yourselves. Eat all the ice cream you want. I left milk and juices, and here is fifty dollars to buy whatever else you need." There were instructions about feeding the cat and feeding and walking the dog, and everything else was for our enjoyment.

The two weeks flew by much too quickly, and when they were about over, Nenita said to me, "I don't want to go back to that house."

"I don't want to go back there either," I answered, "but where else can we go?"

A couple from North Carolina who were attending the church had written to one of their grandmothers, telling her about us. "They are a young missionary couple from the Philippines," they wrote. "We really feel sorry for them. They love the Lord and are doing a wonderful work, but they have no regular financial support."

From nearly the first day on the island, I had started handing out tracts and testifying everywhere I went. Then I began preaching on the streets. Then I was able to start a ministry in one of the local prisons. The servicemen were helping me by giving me Bibles. In a variety of ways, we were winning souls for the Lord.

The grandmother had been looking for someone to support, and we were amazed when a check for a hundred dollars came. "Tell the missionary," the grandmother had written, "that I will be supporting him every month, though not always with this same amount."

This news was delivered along with the check while we were living in that house on the beach for two weeks. The couple said to us, "If you will just sign the check at the back, we can cash it for you." Then they invited us to their house for dinner.

That night at dinner the wife asked us if we had seen all the sites around the island. "No," I said, "we were living so far out of town that we haven't had a chance to really look around." She agreed to pick us up the following day after her children got out of school. She would drop her husband at the base, and we would all take a picnic lunch and go sightseeing.

Before it was over, that lady had shown us the entire island. She introduced us to the best department stores, and she showed us other places we should be ministering. We became very close friends. She said to us, "If you need anything at all, let us know." The last few days we were staying in the other house, they insisted on having us to dinner every night.

During one of those meals, the couple said to us, "If you have no place to go, you can stay here with us."

I said, "Well, that's very kind of you. Thank you very much, but there are three of us, and we would not want to intrude on your home life."

"We have extra room," they insisted. "You're going to stay with us." We gratefully accepted.

The night the owner of the house we were sitting was to arrive, Nenita was cleaning the house and I was mowing the lawn when the pastor came by. He wanted to tell me about another missionary who had been showing evangelistic films around Guam and other neighboring islands, and he wanted me to go meet the man right that minute. I tried to explain to him that we had to get the house ready for the return of its owner, and we didn't have long to do it.

"I understand," he said, "but this man and his whole family are leaving tonight for four weeks to attend an important conference. They need someone to look after their house and their German Shepherd dog. The brother is also looking for someone to rewind his films and place them on another reel, and he is willing to pay for the service."

"I know how to do that," I said, "grateful for my experiences at Bethel Temple."

"Good," he said, "but you need to come over now so that he can show you what he wants done." So, we had a house, and we didn't need to live with someone else.

It was a large house, and the missionaries left us their car to use as well. "Here are the keys," they said, and they were off.

"Praise the Lord," I said to Nenita, "this is great."

I had told the missionaries that they didn't need to leave any money for us, but they did anyway. "This is for groceries," they had said, but we had plenty of groceries already. All we had to do was call our friends and they would bring us over whatever we needed. And we had been invited out to eat so often that we had not yet touched the food in the freezer.

The missionary offered to pay a certain amount for each film that I could finish. I told him that this was our ministry, and I would enjoy doing it. He didn't need to pay us.

It was a fun place to stay. A major park was not far away, and we enjoyed going there. The time passed quickly, especially since the missionary family unexpectedly arrived back home a week early. They had received word that someone was coming to visit one of their works on another island, and they needed to make arrangement for the upcoming meetings.

They insisted that we should not move, that the house was large enough for all of us, and that we could stay in the room we were occupying, but I didn't feel right about doing that. We had a little money, and we needed to find a place of our own.

When the man at the first house had returned, he insisted on giving us an extra $50 for the good care we had taken of the animals, we hadn't spent the $50 left to us for groceries at the second house, the grandmother from North Carolina had sent us $100, and we had received another letter from Lloyd Baker. He said, "The Lord has been good to us, and we would like to encourage your heart. Keep up the good work." Enclosed was another check, this one for $35.00. I had answered the first letter and told him of some of the things the Lord was doing in the ministries we were involved with. The following day we received another letter from the grandmother, and she sent us $65.

While we were sitting at the second house, I met a Lutheran brother who invited me to speak at a men's breakfast. He asked me to share with the men the story of how we had come to Guam and why. After I did that, they took up an offering for us, and it was $175. One of the men there that day insisted that they wanted to do something more for us. "What do you need?" he asked. I told him that we were fine at the moment because we were house-sitting.

"If we find our own place, then we will need some cooking utensils. We have only one cooking pot." The people of the Assemblies church had given us plates, cups, saucers, spoons and everything else we needed except pots and pans. He asked for our address and suggested that he and his wife might visit us. They came one day with a big box full of pots and pans.

We agreed to stay on for a few days with the other missionaries, but I felt restless about staying longer. If they received unexpected guests, they would need the space. Nenita and I decided to sit down and count our money and see what we could afford. We were amazed to find that, although we had landed in Guam with only $64, we now had nearly a thousand dollars. We could afford our own place, since rents were cheap in Guam during those days.

During that last week we were staying with the other missionaries, the pastor called one day in the middle of the week to say that he had something he wanted to speak with me about after the service on Sunday. He would be having a special board meeting, and after that we could talk, if I was willing to wait for a few minutes. I told him I was glad to do it.

I had become more involved with the church. Aside from my activities outside the church, I had been teaching a Sunday school class for a while now, and I was also leading the service sometimes. I enjoyed all of the ministries I was involved with, and I wondered what the pastor had in mind.

After the board meeting was over, he called me into his office and told me that the church janitor had resigned, and they hadn't had anyone to clean the church for the past two weeks. Try as they might, they had not been able to find a replacement. The emergency board meeting had been for the purpose of discussing hiring Nenita and me as their janitors.

I was a little taken aback by this proposal. I knew I had not come to Guam to be a janitor, but I always loved to do whatever was needed in the church. "I would be glad to clean the church," I told him, "but you don't need to pay me anything. I would consider that part of my ministry. I help to make it dirty, so I can help to clean it up."

He said he appreciated my offer, but they would want to pay me so that we could have a decent income and afford a better place to live. But I was adamant. "I cannot accept a salary for that work. This is the House of the Lord, so that's part of our ministry."

"Well, then," he said, "if you don't want to take the money, maybe we could rent you an apartment as our way of showing our appreciation. Look for something you like, and we'll make the monthly payments."

"I have been looking for a place," I told him, "and I think I may have found it. We met a Filipino lady who told us her neighbor had a one-bedroom apartment with a nice living room for rent. It's fifty dollars a month, and I think we'll take it. We have been thinking about moving there on Monday."

"Then let us pay the rent," he said. So that's what we did.

Nenita and I enjoyed our work as janitors of the church. We cleaned the sanctuary each Wednesday in preparation for the Wednesday night service and each Saturday in preparation for the Sunday services.

The couple whose grandmother had begun to support us knew that we had no furniture to speak of, so they gave us tables, chairs, lamps, a radio, a tape recorder, and a television, and they also gave us two sets of their grandmothers' antique china. Then they went out and bought us a bed. They told us to let them know if their was anything else we needed.

The house was practically furnished by that one couple. They also helped us buy a larger refrigerator and a freezer so that we could bring home everything we had stored in the other house. We were very happy! God had showed us His abundant love .

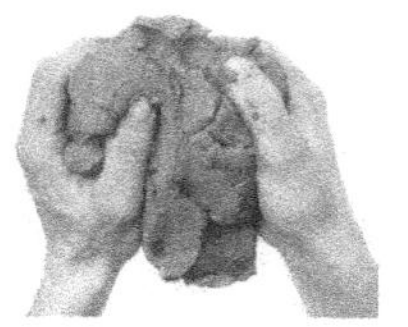

21

ANOTHER SERVICEMAN IN THE CHURCH, WHO LIVED IN A BASEMENT apartment, asked us to start a Bible study in his house, too. This was not just for military people. We continued Bible studies for those living in the barracks, but these were for families in the housing areas. Every now and then the people would give us an offering from these Bible studies.

I was also continuing my prison ministry, I was being invited more to speak to outside groups, and my commitment to the church was stronger than ever. We were busy and about to get busier.

We had been cleaning the Assemblies of God church only two weeks when I was approached by the pastor of the Baptist church, located a block and a half up the hill, and asked if I could help them too. Their church was being cleaned by volunteers, and sometimes it was not well done.

This was a bigger church, with a congregation of some two hundred people. They wanted us to clean their church each Saturday, and they were offering to pay us $150 a month. I said, "We'll do it. When do you want us to start?"

He said, "This Saturday." So, that Saturday and each Saturday afterward, we first cleaned our own church, and then we cleaned the Baptist church. In both, we cleaned the sanctuary, the grounds, the Sunday school rooms, and the bathrooms. Both churches were happy with our work, and often some of the people would give us extra offerings. Some came by while we were cleaning and put money in our pockets, as their tip.

Lloyd Baker had not been able to send any more checks, but his sister-in-law, Ruth Hurd, sent us two offerings. She said she couldn't promise us anything, but that she would send something when she was able. By then, however, we were already comfortable and didn't have any pressing needs. We felt like rich people.

For months at a time, we didn't have to buy any groceries except for milk and juice. Everything else was given to us. People stopped by regularly and brought us things, even fruits, cakes and ice cream.

There came a time when Nenita said to me, "I feel crowded in here. We need to look for a larger place." Joy, now more than two, needed her own room. We were doing well. So, why not?

We spoke with a successful Filipino Realtor and asked if he had any apartments for rent. He said he did and would give us a good price. We went to look at one that had two very big rooms on the second floor. He said he could give them to us furnished if we wanted, but we told him we had plenty of furniture already. This apartment normally rented for $175, but he offered it to us for $125, and we took it. He didn't charge us any deposit.

We still didn't have a car, so we had to rely on a friend to help us move. The pastor helped too, and when he saw where we were moving, he said the church wanted to increase their help to us another $50. I told him we didn't need it because we were only paying $125.

Nenita and I felt secure. We had our monthly rent from the $150 the Baptist Church was paying us. From their payment, we still had $25 left for utilities, plus we had already saved quite a bit. This led us to think seriously about buying a car.

We had known all along that our ministry would never seriously expand without a vehicle, and now we set about to find one. Among the Filipinos who were worshiping at our church, one of them said he had a friend who was selling his car. It was a red 1969 Rambler, "in excellent condition," he said. "If you want to, you can look at it. If you do decide to buy it, he will sell it to you for $35."

I couldn't believe what I was hearing. We had to look at that car, and we decided it was certainly worth $35, so we bought it. This was a big step. We had been walking from our house to church, about a fifty-minute walk going and coming. I had been depending on someone else to get me to my prison ministry, and sometimes they failed me. Now we had our own car.

Having a car elevated us to a whole new status on the island. Now people said, "My, God is really blessing you!" The man who had sold me the car felt badly for not having done anything for us, so he gave me back the $35, and the car was essentially free. Gasoline was still very cheap, so it didn't cost us much to operate it. Life was good in the sun of Guam.

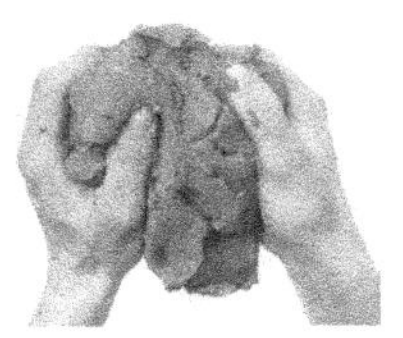

22

AFTER NENITA BECAME PREGNANT WITH OUR SECOND CHILD, SHE was unable to help me with the janitorial work, and it suddenly became too much for me. I called the Baptist pastor and told him he needed to find someone else.

"How about if I increase your salary?" he asked.

"Thank you for that offer," I answered, "but it is not the money. My wife is expecting, I'm doing more and more in my own ministry, and I am still heavily involved in our church. I teach Sunday school, and sometimes I preach when the pastor has to go away. I need more time for my study, and I'm afraid that I might not do a good job at anything." I resigned and began to concentrate more on ministry.

There was another Assemblies of God church at the other end of the island, and I had become involved there too. I was leading Bible studies in the homes of some of their Filipino families. Still, I felt an uneasiness in my soul. We needed to do something more for the Lord. Was it to start a new church? We were not sure. I wasn't comfortable with that idea. It would seem more like splitting the existing church, and I never wanted to be guilty of that.

We were missionaries, and sometimes missionaries start churches, but usually they just help existing churches. We were ready to continue with the existing churches, but we needed to find the exact direction the Lord wanted us to take. Where did He want us in the mix of leadership?

"Lord," we were praying, "what is Your purpose for us in the days ahead? What will be the scope of our ministry here on this island?"

I had become good friends with another missionary. Sometimes we accompanied him to other islands and assisted him in his ministry. Often, usually twice a week, he would invite us to dinner as a way of rewarding us for what we were doing to help them. I got more and more involved with his ministry, and I was really enjoying it.

By the time Nenita was five or six months along in her pregnancy, the people of the church had already told us, "Don't buy anything for this baby. When the time comes, we will have a baby shower." Mrs. Tillman and the couple whose grandmother was supporting us said they would give us anything and everything we needed.

The couple had a crib they wanted to give us, and they said they wanted to buy an infant seat and a stroller for us too. "We'll even give you diapers," they said. "Don't worry about a thing."

When it became apparent that two or three separate baby showers were being planned by different people, I suggested that they all make an effort to get together and have just one. They thought this might be difficult since several churches were involved, so we ended up with two or three of everything.

We found a good doctor, a Catholic believer, who, when he learned that we were missionaries, decided to charge us only for the delivery. All the other visits to his office and his other work at the hospital would be free. Now that we had money and were not worried about it, we didn't have to spend much.

When I had resigned from my work at the Baptist church, Nenita had been a little concerned about how we would make it financially, but just two weeks after I quit that job, the pastor of the Assemblies church where we were worshiping invited me to have lunch with him at a restaurant. He said he had something he wanted to discuss with me. We had been bringing many Filipinos to the church, and I imagined it might have something to do with that.

That day at the restaurant, he began to share his heart with me. "I wanted you to be one of the first to know that we are moving back to the States," he began. "We have been here now for many years, and we feel that it's time for us to go." Their youngest daughter had already moved to the States to begin college, and that may have had something to do with their decision. They had already set a date for their departure (very soon) and had begun shipping some of their personal belongings to the States. They would be working in a Bible college in California.

What he said to me next came as a shock: "I want you to take over the church and move into the parsonage," and he proceeded to hand me keys to everything. "We will have a final farewell service, and then we will be leaving. It's all yours." Amazingly, he and his wife had already moved to a hotel. "Let's go pick up your wife and tell her the good news," he said. When Nenita heard it, she cried.

WOW! I had a lot to do, and fast. I had to notify our landlord that we would be moving. We had signed a one-year lease, but we needed him to release us from that early. He agreed because he was so happy for us.

The parsonage was a mobile home, but it was nice, and it was situated on the beach, just steps from the water. I later told Nenita,

"My, what a beautiful swimming pool we have!" There were two large air-conditioned bedrooms, a built-in washer and dryer and a microwave, among the many appliances. The existing furniture in the parsonage was very nice, so suddenly we didn't need the furniture we had used in our apartment. Over the coming days, we found others who needed it and gave it all away. We had been the janitors of the church for just over six months, and suddenly we had become the pastors. It all seemed like a fantasy.

Nenita had no complications with this child. A boy, he was born in a local hospital, and then he and Nenita came home to our parsonage. For years, I cried every time I thought about all of this. The Lord had promised to prosper us, and He had done it marvelously.

We had gone to Guam toward the end of 1971. We had not been there long when God began to bless us. Before a year was out, we were doing very well. Now, we were prospering. We were able to sponsor my mother, and she arrived to live with us in time for the birth of our second child.

When I first learned that Nenita was pregnant, I had been concerned. Her first pregnancy had been so difficult. I went to the church one night and prayed, "Lord, very few times in my life have I asked You for specific things. Please help Nenita with this pregnancy, and this time I really want to have a boy."

I was kneeling at the altar of the church, and suddenly God showed me a vision. I saw Nenita's womb open, and inside was a baby boy. The Lord said, "Name him David Paul."

I jumped to my feet and drove back to the house. When I arrived, Nenita was ironing clothes. I said to her, "Honey, I have good news for you. God showed me in a vision that it's going to be a boy, and He told me that his name will be David Paul."

"Well, praise the Lord," she said. She, too, had been praying for a boy.

After the baby was born, the doctor came out to the waiting room. He said, "Well, Reverend, congratulations. It's a ..."

I said, "Stop! It's a boy, right?"

He said, "Yeah, it's a boy. How did you know?"

I said, "Because the Lord showed it to me in a vision."

It was August of 1972 and things were going very well for the Llarena family.

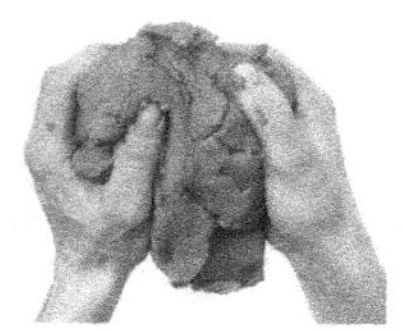

23

THE CHURCH IN GUAM GREW SO MUCH SO FAST THAT WE DECIDED to build an addition. It would extend the sanctuary and also give us additional Sunday school rooms. Many more Filipinos were attending, and we had become crowded. About that time, a desire came into my heart to make a visit to Hawaii.

Some years before, back in the Philippines, I had met a pastor from Hawaii. He handed me his card and said, "When the Lord opens the door for you to come to Hawaii, look me up, and I will have you preach in our church." I had kept that card.

I wrote the pastor in Hawaii and told him that I was now living and pastoring in Guam, but that I would like to visit Hawaii. "Do you still want me to preach in your church?" I asked. "Let me know if you are interested."

He wrote me back and asked me to send him possible dates for a one-week revival meeting in his church. He imagined that such a meeting would open other doors to me in Hawaii and that it wouldn't be difficult for me to fill several weeks. I called him and told him that I could be there after Independence Day and that I would plan to stay about two weeks.

I had a brother in the church from Oregon, a layman who was sent to manage the local Pepsi-Cola plant. He was a powerful speaker, and I asked him to fill in for me while I was away.

The one-week revival meeting in Hawaii was powerful, and through it, I received other invitations. The next two weeks I was busy on service days, but not the other days of the week. But that third week, a Filipino pastor asked me to come to his church, also for a one-week meeting, and he invited me to stay in his house.

Two weeks had now turned into a month. I was in constant communication with Nenita, and she told me that the church was doing well in Guam. Little could I have imagined that I would never go back. It happened in this way.

During that marvelous series of meetings, the pastor and I often had time to talk. He was curious about my background and how I got to where I was in the ministry, and I shared everything with him. Then one day he said to me, "Pastor Ray, I don't consider myself to be a prophet, but somehow in my heart, I don't think you will be going back to Guam."

I found his words to be a strange confirmation. In the weeks I had been in Hawaii, the burden for Guam had somehow lifted from my heart. I was praying for my people in Guam and my family every day, but I no longer had that burning desire to minister there. I told him how I was feeling, and he said, "Well, let's pray about it," and we prayed together there in his living room.

When we had prayed, I said to the pastor, "As always, I am ready for whatever the Lord shows me."

"It would be wonderful if the Lord sent you to work with us here," he said. Later, he told his congregation, "Let's pray for Pastor Ray that God would speak to his heart. We both feel that his time in Guam is over, and maybe he could work with us here in Hawaii." The people prayed, and some of them were very excited about the idea.

When our meetings with that pastor were finished, he told me that I was welcome to stay with them as long as I wanted and that I could make their home my base of operations. I had some other invitations to fill in Honolulu. "After you have finished there," he said, "if you have nowhere else to preach, come back and preach for us." Then he said something more far-reaching: "Why not call for your wife and children to come. We'll help you pay for the tickets."

"Really?" I said, "You would do that?"

"We would be happy to," he said, "and your family can be accommodated here." A plan was forming in my mind. All of this was no coincidence.

Soon afterward, I was invited to preach in another Hawaiian church. The pastor had died, and his wife had taken over the ministry, and she desperately needed an assistant. They had an apartment with two large rooms downstairs, and they offered this to us if my family could come there, and I could help the church.

In the end, I said to the other pastor, "The church pastored by the lady desperately needs help. You have many good workers in your church. I think they need my help more. I can also come and help you sometimes." He agreed, and I sent for Nenita and the children to come.

We had sold the Rambler and bought a new Datsun, and now Nenita had to sell that. She was in a hurry, so she sold it very cheap. She packed up as much as she could in suitcases, asked our friends in Guam to help us ship a few other things, and then she gave the rest away. We had been apart too long.

A humorous thing happened while we were in Hawaii in 1978. When I was preaching in Honolulu, one of my teachers from BBI was sitting on the front row. She had been my chief antagonist at school. After the meeting, she asked to speak to me. "I need to apologize to you," she said.

"Oh," I said, "for what?"

"I was one of those who thought you could never make it in ministry," she said.

I was very touched by her apology. God is so good.

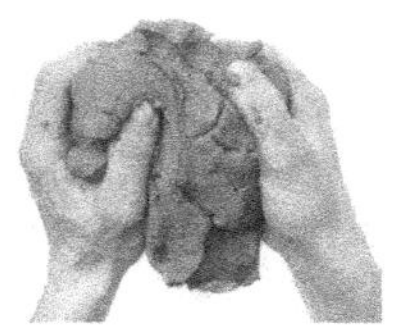

24

After being together in Hawaii for five months, preaching here and there and assisting the lady pastor in her church, one day I said to Nenita, "Somehow I feel in my heart that this is not really the place God wants us indefinitely. The ministry here has been good, but there is something more for us on the mainland." Where exactly I did not know, but I was sure of it.

In the meantime, my sister had married an American serviceman, had moved to the States and was living in North Carolina. We decided to visit her.

It was a long way from Hawaii to North Carolina, and we had to pass by California. I remembered meeting a man who was pastoring in San Francisco, and he had invited me to come and visit him, but somehow I had lost his card. His church was connected to the first church in which I had held a revival meeting in Hawaii, so I asked the pastor there if he knew the pastor in San Francisco and if he had his address or phone number. He did, and I called him and told him we were thinking of coming his way.

"When are you coming?" he asked.

"I am feeling that I should do it soon," I replied.

"Good," he said, "come and stay with us."

"But I'll have my wife and two children with me," I told him. "We're on our way to visit my sister in North Carolina."

"That's fine," he said. "Come and preach some revival meetings for us."

The more I thought about it, the more uncomfortable I felt about taking the whole family into that pastor's home, so I decided that I would send Nenita and the children on to North Carolina to stay with my sister while I preached in San Francisco. They would be comfortable with our family until we decided where God wanted us permanently.

I had another contact in California. Years before, a young evangelist named Al Smith had been sent out by Lester Sumrall to make a trip through the Far East. He visited Hong Kong and came to Manila for some weeks. During that time, we had become good friends. Nenita washed Al's clothes, and we invited him to our house for dinner. Once, when his money had not arrived on time, we blessed him with an offering.

After the services at Bethel Temple, he and I would walk together in Luneta Park. The nights were cool, and we cavorted like children together in the park. We also did something very serious there in that park: we prophesied to each other.

I said to him, "Not long after you get back to the States, you will be married."

He said to me, "The day is coming when you, too, will come to the United States."

These things had been spoken almost in a joking way, but God knew what He had in mind. This had been in January of 1970.

After Al went back to the States, we kept in touch by mail. I had written to him from Guam and said, "Now, it has been proven that you are not a false prophet. Your prophecy has come true. I'm now living in Guam (a protectorate of the United States)."

Not long after that, I received his answer. "Well, you are also not a false prophet. I just got married."

We continued our correspondence. I wrote him from Hawaii that I didn't feel that we should stay on there indefinitely and that I would be planning a trip to the mainland sometime in the near future. I told him my feeling, that I would be moving to the mainland, although I wasn't sure where.

In Al's response, he told me that he was living in Oklahoma City and pastoring a small church there. He also told me that his parents were in San Diego, where his father was pastoring, and he was sure they would want me to visit them there. "Let me know when you're heading that way," he said. "Maybe you could stay and help Dad. You could even develop a Filipino congregation there in his church. There are many in the community around him."

I had never met Al's father, but this thought excited me. We decided to go to San Diego first, and it was arranged that Al's father would meet us at the San Diego Airport late one night.

San Diego was bigger than the towns in which we had been living in Hawaii and a whole lot bigger than anything in Guam. *How will we find Al's father?* I wondered. We had never seen a photo of him.

I wasn't worried. If we missed him, we could take a taxi to a local hotel, spend the night, and sort it all out the next day. Landing in a strange city at night, however, always poses some questions in one's mind.

In that huge airport, my eyes were drawn to a man leaning against a wall. He had on a bright red sweater. Somehow I thought that this was the man I was looking for, and I approached him. "Are you Pastor Smith ... ," I started to say, but at the very same time, he asked, "Are you Ray?" We rejoiced to have found each other so easily. Pastor Smith took us to his house, and we stayed with him for the next month.

I had another contact in San Diego. Before leaving Hawaii, I had spoken with the pastor where I held the first revival meeting and asked if he knew a certain pastor from the same organization in San Diego. He did, we called him, and he, too, had invited me to come for meetings. "Let me know when you get to San Diego," he told me, "and we'll set up some meetings." I had done that, and I enjoyed ministering for that church as well.

That pastor was teaching in a Bible school, and I was also invited to speak at the school—in his classes and in the chapel services. Another pastor, who heard me speak in the chapel services, invited me to preach in his church too. I was suddenly very busy in San Diego and didn't go on to San Francisco for about a month. Nenita and the children stayed with me.

When things slowed down a bit in San Diego, I called the pastor in San Francisco and offered to go there. "Let's have a one-week revival meeting," he said, "and see how things go. Maybe you could also hold a seminar for the workers in our church in the daytime."

I made arrangements to go, but this time I felt that Nenita and the children should definitely go on to North Carolina. I called my sister and asked her what she thought. "Why don't you just move here," she said, "at least until you know where you want to settle." I liked that idea. At least my family would not be shifted here and there, while I found my place in the Lord's harvest field. So Nenita and the children flew to North Carolina and my sister met them there, and I flew on to San Francisco.

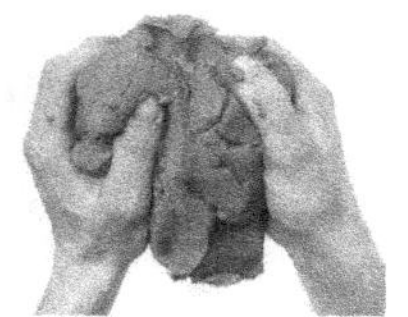

25

I STAYED WITH THE PASTOR IN SAN FRANCISCO AND HELD THE one-week revival meeting we had agreed on, but no other doors seemed to open to me. One older man whom I met was attending an Assemblies of God church, and he said to me, "Why don't you just stay here? We need a Filipino pastor." I told him I would pray about it.

I had been in Hawaii from July through October, had gone to San Diego in mid-October, and by now it was already November. My sister had invited me to come to North Carolina for Thanksgiving, and I told her I would, so San Francisco seemed to be a dead-end.

The old man was so intent on our coming to San Francisco that he offered for us to live in his home. He was retired, he said, and all of his children had married and had their own homes. "We have plenty of room," he said and kept insisting that I, at least, spend a few days with them.

I was tempted to accept this invitation because I had been wanting to have some dental work done. "Wonderful," he said, "I'll take you to my dentist, and I'll pay the bill for whatever needs to be done. I really feel this is where you belong."

"Let me pray about it," I said, "and I need to speak with my wife too."

As I looked around the San Francisco Bay area, the opportunities for ministry seemed to be endless. There was a huge Filipino community there and not many Filipino churches. The church where I had held the revival had some whites and some blacks, but the majority of the believers were Filipinos. Their pastor was Filipino, although he had been raised in California. Something seemed to be drawing me to this place

I flew to Jacksonville, North Carolina, to spend Thanksgiving with my family. One of the important things I needed to do while I was there was to find a good church where they could worship while I traveled. Since my brother-in-law was Lutheran, my sister had been attending services in his church. I had nothing against the Lutherans, but we wanted a good Spirit-filled church for our children to grow up in.

One of the servicemen we met there told us about an Assembly of God church that was not far away. We went there the following Sunday. I introduced myself to the pastor. He had been a serviceman himself and was assigned in Hawaii. There he had met and married a Filipino lady, raised in Hawaii. After he left the Navy, he entered the ministry. When his wife saw that I was a Filipino, she was excited. There were only two other Filipinos in the congregation.

I explained to the pastor that we had been pastors ourselves, then missionaries to Guam and what had been taking place in our lives since them. He asked me, "How long will you be here in town?"

"I have a feeling," I told him, "that after Christmas I will be moving to San Francisco." Nenita and I had discussed what I was feeling and, although we didn't yet have clear direction, I felt fairly sure that this would be our decision. But we were still praying about the details.

"That's a shame," the pastor told me. "A little later in the year, our district will be having our annual Missions Convention. Every church in the district will be raising funds for missionaries. Maybe you could come back for that and speak in some of our churches. I would be willing to pay your airfare if you could come. We have never had a Filipino missionary before."

I gladly accepted this invitation.

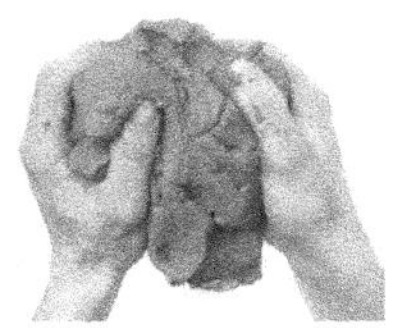

26

Before many days had passed, we became sure of our decision, and I called our friend in San Francisco to say that Nenita and I and the children would be coming after Christmas. "Does your offer still stand?" I asked. "Can we stay with you for a while until we find our own place to live?" He said we could stay just as long as we wanted.

I assured him that we appreciated his hospitality, but one of the first things I would want to do is get my family settled so that I could then think seriously about some ministry in the area.

We flew to San Francisco and stayed with our friend while we looked for some permanent place of our own. One day he told us about another alternative. If we were not completely comfortable with him, he said, his daughter had the entire basement of her house open. It had a bedroom, a bathroom, and a kitchen. "And they have children," he told us, "the same age as yours. Maybe you would be more comfortable with them. At least, your children would have playmates." We accepted this invitation and stayed with his daughter and her family for several weeks while we continued to hunt for our own place.

Again, the pastor asked me to come and preach for him, and this opened meetings in other places. Little by little, I got busy preaching in some of the surrounding areas. There was rarely a Sunday or a Wednesday that I was not preaching somewhere. I had to be careful not to intrude on the time I had promised the churches around Jacksonville, North Carolina.

Eventually, we found a place to rent, although it was much more expensive than we had anticipated. Since we had moved halfway around the world, we again had no furniture, appliances, or dishes. We were starting over from zero. Now, however, our situation was totally different. We had been saving money since we had been so blessed in Guam, then in Hawaii, and now in California. We could go to the store and buy what we needed — or so we thought. We were amazed again when we discovered just how expensive everything was.

I knew that I had some good meetings coming up. The Missions Convention in and around Jacksonville would last for a month, they would pay my round-trip ticket and take care of all of my expenses while I was there, and every church would be giving me an offering. I had upcoming meetings scheduled in Los Angeles and Long Beach, and R.W. Schambach had invited me to come to his church in the Philadelphia area.

We settled on a basement apartment. It had a separate entrance. A large closet was turned into a bedroom, and we put a curtain on the door. There was one large room. Part of it was the living room, and part of it was the kitchen. The bathroom was small, but there was a bathroom. It would cost us $85 a month plus utilities. Thankfully the owners did not ask us to supply any credit references. We had none.

The apartment was not heated, so we had to borrow a space heater until we could buy one of our own. We didn't have much to move, but we decided to move in and then look for the other things we needed. Nenita had a good revelation about this. "Let's not buy anything just yet," she said. "If we do, we will close the door for God to do miracles for us." I agreed fully.

When we were moving out of the house of the young couple, they were led to give us a few things to get us started — some towels and a couple of pots for cooking. The father had a table that he wanted to give and some dishes. There was a stove and a refrigerator already in the apartment, but there was no table. The landlord said, "I'll give you a table."

I had said to Nenita, "The floor is so well carpeted that we can begin to sleep right on it. We have slept in a lot worse places than this."

"I'm certainly not complaining," she said.

That night we moved in, and in the process, I spotted a church just a block away up the hill. It was Friday, and I was sure they would be having a service that night. "There's not much to do around here," I told Nenita. "I think I'll go to the service."

"That's fine," she said. "I want to stay and clean the bathroom, but you go ahead."

It was a youth service and was already in progress when I arrived. It was a beautiful service, and although I didn't know any of the young people present, I felt right at home. After the service, I was able to briefly meet some of the them. I didn't tarry long because I wasn't sure that Nenita didn't need my help with something in our new home.

In one of those brief encounters, one of the young men said to me, "Next Friday night, if you have time, we'd like to invite you to come."

I said, "We'll see." The North Carolina trip was coming up soon, so I didn't have much time to prepare.

I was so happy to get the family settled before I left — in the house and in the church. "Now, I won't worry about anything,"

I told Nenita. "You can easily walk up the hill that one block, and I'll feel better that you're with believers. If any problem should arise, they can help you."

I went to the service that Friday night, and they asked me to introduce myself. The young people were very excited to meet me and to know how close I lived. "Will you help us with our youth program?" one of them asked.

"Well, I'd better not promise anything yet until I get permanently settled," I said, "but I definitely will help. I'm leaving Tuesday for a month in North Carolina. When I come back, I'll see how I can help you."

On Saturday the young people told the pastor that a new preacher had just moved into the community and that he had been a blessing in the youth meeting. He said, "I already noticed him here last Wednesday night. He sat there in the middle of the sanctuary."

On Sunday morning, our whole family went to church together in San Francisco for the first time. We did not get to Community Assembly of God Church for Sunday school, but we did make it for the morning service. Again, the service was in progress as we were coming in.

I was carrying David and Nenita had Joy by the hand. Someone said to Nenita, "Would you like for us to take your daughter to the children's church? And your baby can go to the nursery."

Nenita answered, "I'll keep the baby with me in the service because he doesn't make much noise. If he cries, I'll take him out." The truth was that she felt hesitant to entrust the baby to complete strangers her first Sunday in San Francisco. Joy went along to children's church and enjoyed it.

We sat down in the same place I had sat on Wednesday night, and we began to worship with everyone else. During the course of the worship, there was a time for greeting those around us, and I turned and shook hands with those who were behind us and in front of us.

The next thing I knew, the pastor was motioning in my direction for someone to come forward. Since our signals in the Philippines are somewhat different, I was confused and could not imagine that he was calling for me. We didn't even know each other yet. I looked around to see who he might be calling, and saw no one go forward. Still, each time I looked his way, he would make a motion to me as if he was calling me. I chose to ignore this because I couldn't understand what he could mean.

We all sat down, and the worship leader began making some announcements, but the pastor continued to make his mysterious motion in my direction. Then a lady behind me tapped my on the shoulder and said, "I think the pastor is calling you."

I looked his way, and he did seem to be looking directly at me.

I mouthed the question: "Me?" and he shook his head yes.

I quietly got out of my seat and went forward, climbed the steps of the platform and approached Pastor Ed Stewart for the first time. He gave me a big hug. Then he said, "Would you take the prayer requests?"

I was amazed. We had not yet been introduced, and the pastor wanted to give me a part in the service. I took the prayer requests and led the people in prayer, and then I sat down.

"That was a powerful, powerful prayer," the pastor said. "Folks, with this kind of prayer, how much more powerful must his preaching be. That prayer was anointed. It was prophetic. I can hardly wait for this man to preach. There's something big inside that small package."

I was wondering how the man even knew that I was a preacher when he turned to me and said, "Could you preach for us next Sunday?"

"I'm sorry," I said, "I would love to, but I'm leaving for North Carolina."

"How long will you be gone?" he asked.

"I'll be there for three or four Sundays," I answered, "speaking in various churches for their annual Missions Convention."

"When you come back, can you preach for us?"

"I'm scheduled that week in San Diego," I said.

"Would you let me know when you have an opening because I would like you to come and preach for us here." I assured him that I would do that.

"And don't worry about your family while you are away in North Carolina," he said. Then he asked Nenita to stand and introduce herself, and everyone clapped. "This family has moved in just one block from us," he told the congregation, "and they will be attending our services."

After the service we were met by a flood of greetings, and many said to us, "Tell us what we can do for you." The pastor's wife told Nenita that the women had their ladies' meeting every Wednesday morning, and she invited her to come with the children and share something of her testimony with them. Nenita went and shared with the women of the church, and in the days ahead, they brought all the pots and pans we could possibly have needed.

27

A FUNNY (AND SAD) THING HAPPENED TO US WHILE LIVING IN SAN Francisco. Not every avenue we traveled proved to be blessed, and this was one of those cases.

I was invited to do a revival meeting in a church in Long Beach, California. I had known a Filipino family there, whom I had visited, and they had arranged for me to speak there once before. We took the whole family and caught a Greyhound bus there at our own expense and stayed with our friends there so as to save the church the expense of putting us up in a hotel.

The church was crowded, and every night an offering was taken. Some of the people attending were from other churches where I had spoken over the years. We had called them and told them about the meetings, and they drove there to attend.

We knew that many of these people loved us and were giving in the nightly offerings. The family we were staying with was also attending and giving. I began the meetings on a Sunday night and went right through the following Sunday.

That final Sunday night, the pastor announced, "Pastor Ray has been working hard to bless us, so let's give him a very special love offering. He and his family paid their own fare in coming here, and they have stayed with friends. The church has not incurred any expenses for the meetings other than the advertising we did. Now, we would like to send him home with a special blessing." There was a lot of movement in the place as people went forth and gave their offerings. Nenita, wanting to be blessed, gave $5.00 herself.

After the service, some refreshments were served, and then it was time for us to go. The pastor handed me an envelope, we said our good-byes, and we went to the house where we were staying. Once there, we had some snacks, talked about the people who had been blessed in the services, and it was time for us to go to bed.

"Open the envelope," Nenita said. "See what's in it." I opened the envelope and glanced at the check. It looked to me like $1,980. "Oh, Honey, it's a wonderful offering — $1,980," I said. We were excited and praised the Lord. But for some reason I looked at it again. Only then did I notice that I had been mistaken. It was not for $1,980; it was for only $1.98.

"We'd better go back there," Nenita said. "This has to be a mistake."

But I said, "No."

She told the family where we were staying, and they said they had given no less than ten dollars a night. "Where did my ten dollar offerings go?" the man asked. "We'd better go back there. This has to be a mistake."

But again I said, "No." I didn't want to make a point of the offering. My ministry had never been for hire. If $1.98 is what they gave me, then $1.98 is what we would receive.

"But," Nenita said, "we don't even have money to get home. This isn't enough to buy a one-way ticket on a Greyhound bus. You need to go back there, Honey. This is not right."

"I'm not going back there," I said. "Let's just forget it. The Lord will take care of us."

Eventually, the family we were staying with decided to take us on a trip to San Diego. "Let's drive over there and go to the zoo," they said. "Your kids will enjoy it. It's not that far, maybe two hours."

"If we're going to San Diego," I said, "we could call a friend where I preached there before, and maybe he would like to have me for some meetings." But how could we reach him?

The Filipino lady I knew in Long Beach had married an American serviceman by the name of Brown, and Brown is such a common name that we wondered how we could ever find them. We looked in the Yellow Pages, and there were many pages of Browns. Where should we start?

We decided to at least try, and we called the first several Browns on the list. On the third or fourth Brown we called, my friend answered. We had found them, they put us in touch with the pastor of the church, and he said they were going to have an international banquet and would love for us to be part of that. "Please come," he said.

We drove to San Diego and went to the zoo, and then we went to the meeting that night. The pastor asked me if I would stay and preach that Saturday night, but I didn't have any suitable clothes with me. The man who had brought us said he would take my family back to his home in Long Beach, get some of my clothes, and bring them back the next day in time for me to get ready for the service. And that's what he did.

My family went back to Long Beach with our friends, and I stayed and preached Saturday night and then Sunday morning and Sunday evening. God blessed the people, and He also blessed me. The offering from one service was $800 and from another $1,500, and others had placed money in my hand. When I totaled all up, it was $2,950.

"See, Honey," I said to my wife later, "God has rewarded us." We were able to fly home with money to spare. After that $1.98 check had come, our friends with whom we were staying had given us a few dollars for pocket money for the trip to San Diego. Now, God had blessed us bountifully.

But the story didn't end there. When we got back to San Francisco, I deposited the $1.98 check that we had received from the church in Long Beach, and very soon received a Insufficient Funds notice and a debit of $5 to my account. I couldn't believe that a church would be so irresponsible as to do that to a visiting minister.

But the worst was yet to come: The man at the bank told me that I could redeposit the check if I wanted to and, foolishly, I decided to do that. Then, before long, I received another notice. The check had bounced again. This time the notice was not Insufficient Funds. It was, instead Account Closed. The bank manager lamented my loss of $10 because a church had given me a bad check.

I found that experience to be so distasteful that as I left the bank that day, I tore the check up into tiny pieces and threw it into the air. How could anyone be so irresponsible?

As always, although men were sometimes irresponsible, God was always faithful and kept us.

28

THE PASTOR IN JACKSONVILLE HAD BOOKED ME INTO NONSTOP MEETINGS, beginning with his own church, and my time with him was very fruitful — in more ways than one. He had a prosperous congregation, and they had what they called a "commissary" right there in the building. One day the pastor said to me, "I want you to come with me to the commissary." I wasn't sure what a "commissary" was, but I was willing to go along.

On the way to the "commissary," the pastor explained to me what a "commissary" was. People donated items that might be useful to missionaries. When any missionary came, they were allowed to look though those things and pick out anything they needed. Then the items they selected would be shipped to them wherever they served.

"Pick out anything you would like to have," the pastor told me, "and we'll ship it to you in San Francisco."

I was amazed when I saw what was being offered. There was Tupperware of all sizes and shapes, silverware, towels, blankets and linens, toys, and clothes. Many of the items were brand new and still had the tags on them. He explained that many local companies also donated things and that wealthy members actually bought new items just to be donated.

I called Nenita and told her excitedly, "Two large boxes of blessings are on their way to you. Keep an eye out for them."

The meetings in the other churches were well attended, and the offerings were phenomenal. I preached one Sunday in a church in Kingston, North Carolina, while the pastor was away. God moved so mightily that they asked me if I could come back on the following Wednesday night and preach again. I told them that I wasn't in control of my itinerary and that they would have to call the pastor who had set it all up.

He agreed for me to go, but I had to be in another church for Sunday and the following Wednesday. That night, the Spirit of the Lord moved mightily in that place, and the service was powerful. They had been traversing some problems that I knew nothing about, but the Spirit addressed them.

The pastor's wife was in tears. "You have just really hit our problem on the head," she said. "Your visit has been a blessing and a comfort to us." I spent the night in that place, and the pastor's wife drove me halfway to my next appointment the next day. The pastor where I would be preaching that night came that far to get me.

When the pastor came home, his wife told him what God had done on Sunday morning and Wednesday night. "We need to get this man back here," he said. "He has the answer to some of the problems we've been going through." He and his wife drove to where I was speaking that night and asked me to come to their church for revival meetings. I explained that my schedule was full while I was there, but he said, "Well, after you finish those commitments, couldn't you come to us before you go back home?" I couldn't because I had other appointments in California.

I did later go back to that church for a great revival meeting, and it was through those people that another wonderful door would open to me. These friends were originally from the Michigan District of the Assemblies of God.

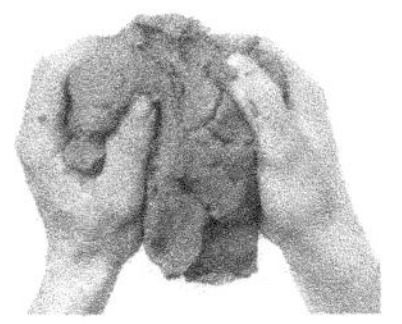

29

WHEN I GOT BACK TO THE CHURCH IN SAN FRANCISCO, PASTOR STEWART said to me, "We would like you to be a part of our team here. Why don't you join my staff?" I told him that I had too many things going on at that moment. I would gladly help him, but I wasn't in a position to become part of the staff. I still wasn't sure of the direction the Lord was taking us in California and had no idea how long we would be staying there.

We were involved in the church as much as possible. Nenita and the children attended every week, and I went when I was in town. Usually, Pastor Stewart asked me to preach on these occasions. Sometimes, when he wanted to leave town for vacation, he would arrange with me ahead of time to fill in for him. We quickly became very close friends.

Pastor Stewart asked me if I could help him do visitation to follow up on new leads for the church. I agreed to do that when I was not away preaching. He would give me a list of those who needed follow up, and I would visit them. When some Sunday School teacher was absent, I would be called upon. As he had done on that first Sunday, sometimes the pastor called on me to take prayer requests and lead the people in prayer. Slowly, my involvement increased.

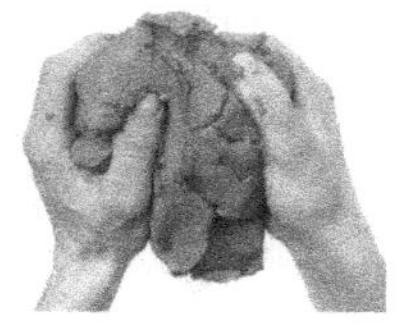

30

Our next child (and the last), Leah, was born in San Francisco in 1974. By this time, David was already three years old, and I told Nenita that we needed to find a larger apartment. I was having meetings in which I received offerings, and the church was paying me something for the work I did for them.

I found an available apartment just two blocks from the church on another street. The rent was $195, plus utilities. We felt we could afford the move. People gave us more furniture, and we lived in that apartment for the next two years.

Now that the family was growing, it bothered me to be on the road so much. When the church offered to give me a raise, put me in charge of the Christian Education Department, and give me an office, I decided to accept their offer. I needed to settle down a little, so I accepted fewer invitations to preach far away. I took a few trips to other cities, and I still spoke in Stockton, Sacramento, and the Los Angeles areas, but when I did, I took the whole family along.

I also made two mission trips to Ecuador. Over the years, I had lost contact with the McDougals, but somehow in 1975, I learned that they were in Ecuador and that five Filipino missionaries were working with them there, operating a camp outside of Quito. People were coming from all over South America to be blessed. It sounded so wonderful that I immediately wanted to be part of it. I knew that if I went to Ecuador, I would not be generating money while I was there, but I also knew that God was able to take care of me and of my family in my absence. I trusted Him. I went and was not disappointed.

For the next month, I was busy in that beautiful Andean nation in meetings. We preached in the camp outside of Quito, and then we preached in and around the city and other cities. One day, around noontime, we were preaching in one of the most important plazas of the capital city, just in front of the famous San Francisco Church. It was a very tense time in the nation because the presidency had recently been threatened by a coup.

A small group of camp people accompanied me. Someone brought a guitar so that we could sing, and one brother went along to interpret for me. It was great fun. The people listened intently to what we said, and they were such interesting people.

We drew such a crowd that a policemen eventually came along and asked us to stop. We moved to another part of the park and kept on preaching. Revival was on in Ecuador, and it was a very exciting time to be there.

When I got back to San Francisco from a preaching trip to Hawaii, there was a letter waiting from Brother Harold asking me to come and preach for them. As I read it, I got very excited and decided I needed to go.

Nenita was not nearly as excited about the idea. "We have no money for you to go," she insisted. "The children are growing, and our needs are growing too. I don't see how you can possibly go. The offering you received in Hawaii was just enough for us to survive on until the next meeting. What you're receiving from the church is not enough."

I understood what she was saying, and I was not accustomed to doing rash things, but I really felt that I should go. When I tried to convince her, however, she insisted, "No! No! No!" Her opposition to my going on that trip was so strong that we didn't speak about it again until the time drew near for me to leave.

As that time drew near, another complication arose. Leah got very sick. Her ears were infected, and she was running a high fever. Our pediatrician told Nenita that he needed to do surgery to drain the ears or they might rupture and leave Leah with a permanent disability. He scheduled the surgery, and it fell within the days I would be gone. When Nenita came home with this news, she was sure this would cause me to cancel my plans. But I said, "No, I can't cancel."

"But you have no ticket," she said.

"I know it," I told her, "but I need to go. They are expecting me and the meetings are set up."

Then, Nenita got very upset with me. "You don't have any money," she reminded me.

Then I got angry too, and I said, "Get thee behind me, Doubting Thomas." I was sure that going to Ecuador was in the will of God.

"Honey," I told her, more seriously this time and with less anger, "you know the Lord will provide."

"Yes," she said, "but we have three children. Leah needs to have surgery, and we don't even have enough money for that. How can you think of going off to some other country right now?" I knew it didn't make sense, but I went ahead packing my things little by little.

Two weeks before I left, I said to Nenita one day just after lunch, "I'm going to the post office to see if anything has come in." I had rented a post office box in San Francisco because we had moved several times, and it seemed safer to have a permanent address that we could give to everyone, something that wouldn't change if we moved again.

She said, "You just came from there this morning. Why are you going back again so soon?"

"I just feel like I need to go," I said, and I went.

On my way to the post office, I did some serious praying. I said, "Lord, You're the Boss, and I really need a miracle. I know in my heart that I need to go, but I also have some personal needs."

Even before I opened the postal box, I could see something inside that looked interesting and unusual. It was a long envelope with a red, white, and blue pattern on it. I was very nervous as I began to open it.

The envelope was from the pastor in Hawaii where I had just finished the revival meeting. It contained a check, and I had opened the letter in such haste, that I almost tore it in two. The letter said that he wasn't sure what my need was at the time, but that the Lord had been dealing with him and his wife to send me some money. The round-trip fare to Ecuador at the time was only $572.00, and the check was for exactly that amount. I danced for joy.

I ran back to the apartment. Nenita was there playing with David and Leah. "I received a great victory," I told her excitedly, "a check in the exact amount that I needed for my airfare."

Now, she seemed to get a little excited about the trip too, but she was still worried because we had no money. The bill for the surgery would be expensive. But God would provide. I knew it. I went and cashed the check and bought my ticket to Ecuador. When it came time to leave, I had just fifty dollars in my pocket and a few coins.

I had held back $35, and as Nenita and I were praying before I left, I said to her, "Open your hand." She did. "This is all the money I have to leave you," I said to her, placing the $35.00 in her hand.

She looked at the bills. "This is all?" she said, and she was so angry that she was crying.

I put my hand on the $35 and prayed, "God, You are a God of multiplication. You are a God of increase. You have never failed us before. I know in my spirit that this trip is Your will. God, cause this money to multiply. Take care of my family and bless them. Their lives are in Your hands. Don't let anything happen to them while I am away these weeks."

The Sunday before the pastor had made an announcement in the service: "Pastor Ray is leaving for missionary duty in Ecuador. His family will be home by themselves. It is our responsibility to visit Nenita and see how they are all doing. Some of you ladies, visit her to encourage her, and take something with you when you go. If she needs to go somewhere, ladies, drive her."

A dear black sister in the church was a retired nurse. She said to me, "Pastor Ray, I have plenty of time, and I'll take care of your wife. I'll drive her to the hospital when Leah has to go in for the surgery. And I can bring the children back and take care of them while Nenita is with Leah."

"See," I had told Nenita, "everything is arranged," but now that I was leaving her so little money, she was in tears. I called a taxi and left, as much as I hated to leave her that way.

Rarely had I seen my wife in such a mood. "You are a very irresponsible father," she had said to me. "Other ministers would not leave their families in this way."

"Honey, I need to do this," I had answered.

I was crying myself as the taxi headed toward the airport, and I was feeling very heavy. Was Nenita right? Was it just my pride that made me want to go on this trip?

I had to fly San Francisco to Dallas, Dallas to Miami, and Miami to Quito. All the way to Dallas the devil tormented me: "You're worse than an infidel. You're worse than an infidel. Anyone who doesn't take care of his family is worse than an infidel." I was feeling very guilty about that time, and if the plane had been able to turn around, I would have gladly gone back home.

"What kind of man of God are you?" the enemy continued. "Common sense tells you that this is not a good time to leave home. Your daughter is in danger, and you don't even care."

I had a hard time finding my connecting gate in Dallas that day, and it took me a long while to get to the right place for my departure to Miami. I almost didn't care. What was I doing anyway? I was hurting my family, and for what? I was feeling very low as my plane finally took off for Miami.

Just before we landed in Miami, the Spirit of the Lord spoke to me and cleared my thinking. "If you are going to fulfill My assignment and follow My orders, do you dare think that I'm not capable of taking care of your family?" I knew it was a message from Heaven, and by the time we landed in Miami, my spirits were high.

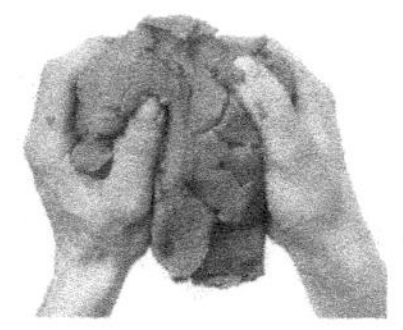

31

My flight to Quito was delayed for several hours, and I had opportunity to speak with other passengers. A lady named Patsy Allen and her companion were also going to Ecuador for missionary work. They were to meet and work with the Assemblies of God missionary, Miguel Santiago. They, too, were very excited about their trip, and we worshiped together there in the Miami Airport.

There was a couple from New York, both professors at one of the universities in Quito. They couldn't speak much English, but with our few words of "broken" Spanish we led the two of them to the Lord while we waited for our flight. In due time, our flight left, and I arrived for my visit in the breathtakingly beautiful nation of Ecuador.

As before, the McDougals kept me busy in all sorts of activities there in and around the camp. In fact, I was so busy in the spiritual activities in Ecuador that I was able to forget about the situation I had left at home. I was doing the Lord's work, and I was sure He would take care of my family. He always had, and I believed He always would.

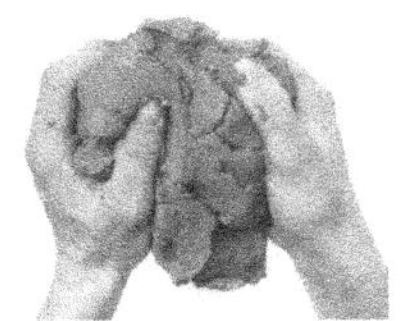

32

By the time I left for home, my money was all gone. I had spent the last few dollars for some souvenirs to take to my family, and when I arrived in San Francisco, I didn't even have change to make a phone call.

It was midnight, but I had no choice. I called home collect. "Honey," I said, "it's me. Do you have any money?"

"Where are you?" she asked.

I said, "I'm at the airport. I can take a taxi home, but I don't have enough money left to pay it. Can you pay the taxi when I get there?"

"I can," she answered.

When I got home, the children were all sleeping, and I told Nenita not to disturb them.

"Are you hungry?" she asked.

"Not really," I told her. "Maybe I'll just have something to drink."

"Well, how was your trip?" she asked me, and I began telling her everything.

Eventually I got around to the surgery. "How did the surgery go?" I asked.

"What surgery?" she said.

I said, "Leah's ear. She was scheduled to go in when I left."

"Oh, my goodness," she said. "I haven't told you." She told me that the black sister, Sister Anderson, had come the next day and taken them for a follow-up appointment with the doctor. He had examined Leah and said that apparently the antibiotic was working and the surgery was no longer necessary. "We were glad for that," she said. "The surgery would have left her with a slight scar." What a blessing!

"But how are *you*?" I asked my wife.

"Let's go to our room," she said, "so we can talk without worrying about waking the children." When we got into the bedroom, she said, "Sit down."

"Okay," I said, wondering what was coming next.

"I'm going to tell you what the Lord has done while you were gone," Nenita said. She opened a drawer, took out an envelope and handed it to me. "Here is the $35 you left me," she said. "I didn't spend a single penny of it, so now I'm giving it back to you."

"Oh, yeah?" I said excitedly.

Then she took another envelope out of the drawer and said, "Here is the rest of the money that came in while you were gone. I'm giving it to you."

I counted the money in the envelope. It was almost $5,000. "Did you rob a bank?" I asked.

"No, not at all," she answered and began to relate to me the story.

I had left her in the morning, and she had still been crying. She sent Joy to school, and was left with David and Leah and our landlord's little girl she was babysitting. She was mumbling to herself and complaining about her life and about me. "If my husband insists on living like this, it can only mean that he is favoring others above us, and I'm not going to let this happen again." She was very upset. She cleaned the house and did the laundry, but all the while she cried and told herself she was going to change things.

She kept thinking about Leah having to go to the hospital the following day. She was still not feeling well. And Nenita was feeling even worse, feeling sorry for herself.

About eleven that morning the doorbell rang, and she opened the door. It was a Mexican lady from the church known to us as Sister Rachel. She said she had been watching Jim Bakker and the PTL Club on television when the Lord spoke to her and told her to visit my family. She turned off the television, got her overcoat, took her bag and umbrella and went out the door.

As she was about to lock the door, the Spirit of the Lord spoke to heart, "Go and get $60 from your drawer." She thought, I'm not planning to do any shopping or to go anywhere else. I'm just going to walk up the hill to the Llarena's apartment. What would I need $60 for?

Just before she arrived at our apartment and greeted Nenita with the usual, "How are you doing today?" Nenita had received a telephone disconnect notice. It stated that if the bill was not paid by the next day, the phone service would be cut. The overdue phone bill was for $60.00, and this only added fuel to Nenita's fire. She was very upset.

So, when Sister Rachel asked Nenita how she was, she answered "Oh, I'm just fine. My husband left a few hours ago for a mission trip, and Leah is sick and has to have surgery. I don't understand why he had to go away right now."

"Well, I'm sure Brother Ray wouldn't go unless he really believed it was of the Lord," she answered. "So, the Lord will take care of it," and she continued to encourage Nenita.

Nenita always loved to sing, and the two of them sang many wonderful songs of praise together that day, and they shared many testimonies of God's goodness together.

Finally, it was time for Sister Rachel to go. "Is there anything else I can do for you?" she asked my wife.

"No, just pray for me," Nenita answered.

"Well, I will, but for some reason I feel like you have a very pressing need you haven't told me about. Your baby's sick and your husband's away, but something else is troubling you. What is it?"

"Well, then look at this," Nenita said, bringing out the disconnect notice. "I have no money to pay it, and the telephone will be cut tomorrow."

"How much is this?" Rachel asked.

"It's $60.00," Nenita told her.

"Well, now I understand why the Lord sent me back inside my house to get $60.00. Here, this $60.00 is for you."

"No," Nenita protested. "I can't take that. I know you don't have much and are living on unemployment. You told the church about being laid off."

"Oh, but I have some savings," Sister Rachel said, "and the Lord spoke to me to go back and get $60.00. So this is for you," and she gave it to Nenita.

While they were standing there talking, Joy came home from school. Rachel said, "It's time for me to go home now, Sister Llarena. But I'll come back sometime next week." Then, as she was going down the stairs, she turned and asked, "How are you going to the office to pay the telephone bill tomorrow?"

"I'll just ride the bus," Nenita answered.

"With three kids?" Rachel asked. "That would be too hard. Just give me the bill, and I'll go and pay it for you."

"Would you really do that for me?" Nenita asked.

"Sure," she answered. "It will be easier for me to ride the bus alone." So, Nenita gave her the phone disconnect notice and returned the $60.00. But Rachel would not receive it. "The Lord told me to give that to you, so you keep it," she said, "I'll pay the phone bill."

The next morning an older couple from the church, the worship leader and his wife, came by and said to Nenita, "Since Pastor Ray is gone, we'd like for you to know that you can call on us anytime you have a need. Don't feel like a stranger, and don't be embarrassed. You are like our children. We're here to help you. You are part of our church family, and we want to take care of you."

Nenita welcomed them in and they were carrying four bags of groceries. "We can't stay long," the wife said. "We have some other places to visit. You'd better put the ice cream in the freezer so it won't melt and the meat, too, so it will keep." They prayed with Nenita, gave each of the children a kiss, and left.

Nenita took the grocery bags into the kitchen and began to put their contents away. In the bottom of one of the bags was an envelope. It contained some cash, about $150.00. When Nenita saw it, she began to cry and asked the Lord to forgive her for her lack of faith.

The following morning Nenita took Leah to the doctor, and that was when she learned that a healing had taken place and the surgery would not be required. The Lord spoke to her and said, "You have been looking to the arm of flesh rather than looking to Me. I am fully capable of taking care of your children, much better than your husband can do it." In that moment, Nenita felt very ashamed for having given me a hard time.

I left on a Monday or Tuesday. That Sunday, when Nenita and the children went to church, many people put money into her hand. When she got home, she opened her Bible and found another

$50.00 that someone had placed inside. She put it aside with the rest. This is why she never had to spend the $35.00 I had left her. Others gave her more than enough money to sustain her and the children during the time I was away.

We lived on the second floor, and one day Nenita was sweeping down the steps. At the bottom of the steps there was a rubber doormat. When she reached the doormat, she found that there was an envelope lying on top of it. It could have easily been blown away by the wind. Someone had written on the envelope "Pastor and Mrs. Llarena." She thought, That was crazy of someone to put this here where it could blow away. They could have at least put it in the mailbox. She dropped it into her pocket and continued cleaning.

Later, when she was back upstairs, she took the envelope out of her pocket and laid it on the table while she washed the dishes. Finally, after having finished the dishes, she sat down at the table and was enjoying a cup of coffee and decided to open the envelope and see what was in it. What she found there was $298.00. There was no note enclosed, and the name of the donor was nowhere to be found on the envelope. To this day, I have no idea where that offering came from.

Before it was all over, Nenita had accumulated nearly $5,000 above her expenses for the month. Every time she went to the church, people put money in her hand. The church gave her an offering to help with the expenses of the home while I was away, and they continued to pay my salary, although I wasn't doing my job at the moment.

When Nenita had finished telling me all this, I said to her, "The Lord has just proven to us that we should always look to Him. He is our Source." Never again did she complain when I went on trips and left the family for some weeks. She knew that God would be with them.

That night she said to me, "We need to buy a piano for Joy. This money could go for that." Joy had been taking piano lessons and sometimes cried because she had nowhere to practice. The next day we went out and bought a piano for Joy and paid cash for it.

"You know what?" I said to Nenita that first night, "I should leave tomorrow and go somewhere else. You are richer when I'm not around."

"No," she said. "Stay for a while, at least for a month."

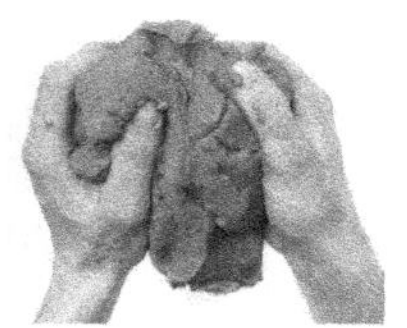

33

THE OWNER OF THE APARTMENT WE WERE RENTING AND HIS WIFE HAD a little girl. Her mother had been baby-sitting for them, but now she needed to go back to work. They spoke with Nenita and asked if she would be willing to care for this child. Nenita was delighted.

They not only paid her for this service, but they also got her involved in selling Avon for them to the church people, and that generated some more income, and I had my income from the church.

One day, after we had been living there for a year, the landlord, who was also a Realtor, came to talk to me. "You are the best tenant we have ever had," he said. "You pay your rent on time. You don't complain. You fix things that you can fix. You never bother us. You're a good tenant, and we would hate to lose you, but I want you to have your own house. Would you like to go around and look at some available houses?"

I laughed. "With what? Can I buy a house with my looks? My income is not sufficient," I'm sure.

He was surprised by this answer. We were always so positive around him. "What happened to your testimony that your God is the God of the impossible?" he said. "Where is He now?" His words were like a slap in the face.

Nenita and I looked at each other. We didn't want God to be seen as small. "Let's go," I told her. "Nobody's forcing us to buy. We'll just look."

We looked at eight houses and found nothing that would have fit our needs. "No more," I said. "It's enough."

But the Realtor was not finished. "This next one is ideal for you," he assured me. "Just look at one more. See if maybe your God will tell you that this is the right house."

"Well, it doesn't cost us anything to look," Nenita said. "We might as well go." So we went.

The house was located just three blocks from the church we were attending, and it *was* beautiful. It sat on a corner lot, so that there was no neighbors on either side. It had a backyard, but the neighbor in back was far enough away that it was no problem. As an added incentive, there were many Filipinos in the neighborhood already.

We liked what we saw from the outside of the house. It was of a semi-Victorian design, and it was well painted. Then, when we walked up the stairs and into the house, we looked at each other. It seemed that a wonderful peace had settled over us.

"This is it!" I said.

"What are you feeling?" the Realtor asked. We had to admit that we were both feeling very good about that particular house.

"You should place a one-hundred-dollar deposit on it," he said, "to secure the sale. If you don't qualify for the financing, all you will lose is $100."

That sounded logical, but for some reason, that $100 seemed to me to be $1,000 about then. "That's about all we have in the checking account right now," I said. But we wrote the check.

When the financing offer came, the bank was requiring a down payment of 10% ($4,400 on the $44,000 purchase) plus closing costs, and that was more than we could raise at the moment.

We loved the house, and we believed it was what the Lord wanted us to have, but we didn't know how to make it happen.

The Realtor said, "Let's figure out a way to make this happen." But I understood the bank's position. My income was not stable. Sometimes there was a lot, and sometimes there wasn't nearly as much. The only stable income we had was from the church, and that wasn't very large yet.

"Do you have any friends who might be able to help you to generate the money?" our Realtor friend asked. "Or could one of your friends buy the house in their name and let you transfer it later into your own name when you qualify?"

"Who would do that?" I wondered out loud.

I had met a couple. He was a Filipino married to an American, and we had become close friends. Sometimes the four of us would go out to dinner together. Other times, they would come to our house and bring their children. When they heard about this situation, the man said, "I would be willing to do that. Four of us are working in our family, and we have our own house already. We could qualify to buy a second home."

"I would find it difficult to ask anyone to do that for us," I told them, "but if you would like to do it, I would appreciate it very much." They filed the application, and it was approved.

Now, I needed to come up with the down payment and the closing costs. The idea was that we were just using our friend's name to secure the loan. The full responsibility for payments would be ours. The Realtor came by and said that the seller would not mind holding the down payment as a second mortgage. Instead of coming up with the full amount, we would pay him over time in monthly installments of $46.00. That was not bad. We could handle that. The payment on the first mortgage, including taxes and insurance, was only $289.60. We decided to buy the house. Now, we just needed to come up with the necessary closing costs.

Until that time, we had not established any credit rating. A lady at the church heard about our predicament and said to me, "I want to help you establish your credit. We will borrow your closing costs at the bank, and I will co-sign the note for you." And she took us to a popular finance corporation.

After they asked me about my income and my assets, it was determined that the loan could be made with this lady as the guarantor or co-signer. If we failed to pay, she would be responsible, and they asked her if she was prepared for that eventuality. She said she understood fully and was willing to pay if we, for some reason, could not make our monthly payment. "I know that God will not fail them," she said. "He is one of our pastors."

As collateral for the loan, they listed our furniture and most everything else we owned (we had no vehicle yet). Finally, I was qualified for a loan of up to $1,800. That was more than enough to cover the closing costs.

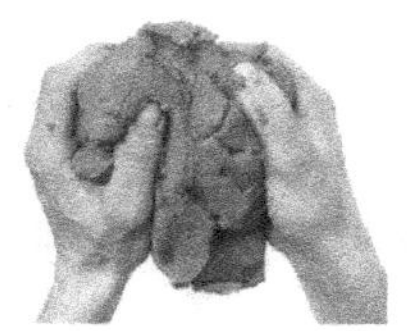

34

After I arrived back from that second trip to Ecuador, Pastor Ed Stewart approached me and asked if I would be willing to work for the church full-time. "I love the church," I told him, and I would be more than happy to work with you more, but I need my liberty. If I would be free to go when there were doors open to me, either in overseas missions or in meetings here in the States, I would accept. I don't do it as much now as I used to, and it wouldn't be every month. I would give you advanced warning of the times I would be away."

He accepted my offer, took me into a full-time position, increased my salary, and moved me into a bigger office. From that time onward, I had much more authority in the church, and I was given liberty to do whatever I wanted to do in ministry outside the church.

In the church, I was mostly involved with the evangelistic outreaches and the Christian Education Department. I still made several trips a year, some of them to preach in a church in Cheboygan, Michigan (never realizing that I would, at some point, be much more involved there). Life in San Francisco was good. We were there for eight and a half years, and we enjoyed that time immensely.

Working with Pastor Stewart was a joy. We had many wonderful times together, times in which we experienced great revival. It was a wonderful relationship, marked by an unusual unity. There was no friction between us, and we had few problems of any kind during those years. Was it to end?

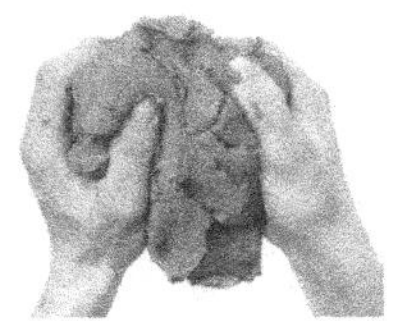

35

When I went back to North Carolina to have that revival meeting, the pastor had told me he wanted me to come back again, but I hadn't heard from him in a long time. One day, in December of 1974, he called.

"Pastor Ray," he said, "you can't imagine what I've been through trying to reach you. I lost the address you gave me. I tried many things to locate you, but I wasn't able to find you. We remembered that you were with the Assemblies of God, and I called their district office in California, but they had no record for you." (I hadn't gotten around to transferring my credentials to California yet.)

This pastor had also called a friend in Missouri and asked him to help find me, but to no avail. Eventually, they had met a missionary coming from the Philippines, and they asked him if he knew where we were living. He knew and gave the pastor our address in San Francisco.

"We have taken a church here in Cheboygan, Michigan, Huron Street Tabernacle," the pastor told me, "and I would like for you to come for a revival meeting. We can send you your airfare if you're willing to come for a week." This was a divine encounter that would eventually bring our whole family to live in Michigan. I liked the people in Cheboygan so much that I began going there two or three times a year.

Then, after some years, the pastor of that church resigned, and the church leaders began looking for a replacement. They didn't have much luck, interviewing candidate after candidate without finding someone they liked. Eventually, they interviewed twenty-three candidates for the pastorate and were not happy with any of them.

Early in this process, I was asked if I would come and pastor the church. The chairman of the board of trustees called me several times. "I'm not interested," I told him. "It's too cold in Michigan for Filipinos. I have no desire to shovel snow all winter long."

Besides that, although I didn't say it to him, San Francisco was a major city, and Cheboygan was a town of twenty thousand people. This seemed like a major step backward to us.

"I'll still come and visit you," I told him, "and I would be happy to come for some revival meetings, but not to be your pastor. No, that's not for me. I'll be praying that you'll find the right man."

But he didn't discourage easily and kept calling me. Sometimes he called two or three times a day. In response, I got more forceful in my answers: "There's no way I'm going to pastor in Michigan," I told him. "You'd better find someone else."

In 1980, we got word that my mother was sick in the Philippines, and we decided to make a visit to our families. Our two youngest children had not been to the Philippines, and we wanted them to meet everyone and see our homeland.

Some members of Bethel Temple had a condominium not far from the church, and they allowed us to stay there free of charge. They lived about four blocks away. One day they came over to tell me that there had been a call from the United States. "Come on over to our place," I was told. "The man said he would call back in thirty minutes."

"I'll be right there," I told them.

It didn't take me long to walk the four blocks to their house, and when the call came, it was the man from Michigan again. I was surprised. "How did you know I was here?" I asked. "And how did you find us? I didn't give anyone this number, not even the church in San Francisco. I told them I would be at Bethel Temple, but I didn't leave them a phone number."

He said he had called the church in San Francisco, and the secretary there had told him that we were in the Philippines. He had called back later and asked if she could give him a phone number, but she only knew the name of the church where we would be staying — Bethel Temple. He had proceeded to call information for Manila and asked for Bethel Temple, and that's how he had found the church number. Then, someone at the church had given them this other number.

"We need you to come and pastor us," the man said. "Forgive me for tracking you down, but we're desperate."

"But I've told you that I'm not interested," I protested.

"Would you please just pray about it before you reject us?" he pleaded.

I said, "I will not pray about this because the Lord is not sending me there."

"But we really believe that you are the man," he continued. Then he told me about the twenty-third candidate they had interviewed.

"I appreciate your call," I said, "but I'm really not interested. I cannot leave San Francisco."

"Will you at least pray about it?" he urged. "Please!"

"Okay," I said, just to get him to stop. "I'll pray about it."

"When do you get back to the States?" he asked.

"After three more weeks," I told him.

"Will you call us when you get back?" he asked.

"I'll call you," I promised, not really meaning it. And when we got back to San Francisco, I did not call Cheboygan. I didn't know what to tell those lovely people. I had no desire whatsoever to be their pastor.

Several weeks went by, and the man called me again. "You promised you would call," he said.

"Well, the truth is that I just didn't know what to say," I admitted. "I'm really not interested."

"The church is fasting and praying for you to come," he told me. "We're having congregational prayer meetings, and everyone is attending. We are all very excited about you coming. Several people already saw you here in visions. One man saw a vision of you wearing a white suit and riding a white horse, and he knew you were coming."

"That's a crazy vision," I said. "When I next make a trip to Michigan, it will not be on a white horse, I can assure you."

"Well," he said, "one lady dreamed that you were standing in front of the congregation preaching. The power of God came down, and the Spirit of the Lord moved."

I said, "That's fine, but the Lord hasn't spoken to my heart." But this was not the complete truth. The truth was that by this time I *was* feeling something for Cheboygan, but I didn't want to admit it or accept it. Life was too good in San Francisco, and I didn't want anything to interrupt that life. My role in the church there seemed to be tailor-made for me by God. It was perfect. I couldn't have asked for anything better.

When I wanted to go somewhere else to preach, the church would take an offering to help pay my travel expenses, and they would always continue paying my salary while I was away. Where could I find a setup to match that? I was having a ball. The church was growing, and we were busy in meetings. I would be crazy to think of leaving all that.

But the man didn't give up. He had started calling me in May of 1980, he had called me that July in the Philippines and now, toward the end of August, he was still calling me. I kept saying the same thing: "No, I don't want to leave San Francisco."

When the pastor in San Francisco learned that someone from the church in Michigan had been calling me, he said, "Over my dead body! I'm not going to let your go. Just tell them to stop calling." He told his secretary, "If these people call again, hand the phone to me. I'll straighten them out."

The church in San Francisco was growing. We had bought a supermarket and were in the process of remodeling it. When the pastor was away, I was responsible for managing the work of renovation. I couldn't have left them, even if I had wanted to. The project was to be completed in the summer of 1981, and an inauguration was set for June.

But toward the end of 1980, I got very sick. I began feeling bad and it worsened, until one day the church secretary came back from lunch to find me passed out on my desk. She was able to revive me and immediately drove me to the emergency room. I protested to the doctor who examined me there, "I'm not really sick. I have just been feeling a little weak and sometimes dizzy."

He couldn't find anything wrong with me. "Maybe you have not eaten well today," he suggested, "or maybe you have not been resting very well. I would suggest that you take a few days off, and I think you'll be fine."

I had told Nenita several times that I was not feeling well, and she had felt my head to see if I had a temperature. I didn't, so there didn't seem to be anything to do.

While I was in the emergency room that day, the man from Michigan called. "Ray's sick, and they have taken him to the emergency room," Nenita told him.

"Oh," he replied jokingly, "the Lord is punishing him because he's not listening to what He's trying to tell him."

"Please don't say that," Nenita objected. "That's not funny."

"Well, tell him to come to Michigan, and we'll nurse him back to health and take care of him," was the reply. "This is where he belongs."

As I was waiting for the emergency room doctor to come and check me, I talked to God. "Lord," I prayed, "if I have done anything to cause myself to be sick, show me what it is. If this is because I am not responding to the invitation to Michigan and You want me to go, I'm willing, but You will have to make it very clear to me that this is Your will. I can't see the advantage of going there."

My greatest concern was having to deal with Nenita because she had already made it very clear to me that she wanted nothing to do with Michigan. She had made many friends in San Francisco, she loved the church and its people, and she was involved in its ministry. She had said to me very clearly, "I do not want to pack up again and move. This is it."

Sometimes, when I had gone to Michigan for revival, I had come back and told Nenita how deep the snow was there, and consequently, she hadn't even wanted to visit there. Not long after the emergency room episode that December, I dared to tell Nenita what I was feeling: "I think the Lord wants us to move to Michigan."

"Well, you'd better be sure," she answered.

After we had gotten back from the Philippines that year, I had petitioned for a visa for my mother to come and live with us. Her paperwork was approved, and she came in January of 1981. By the time she had arrived, I was already fairly sure that I should move to Michigan. The people in the church there had not ceased to call me, and I was feeling more and more like this was indeed the will of God.

When we still proved hesitant, they suggested that we not accept the position sight-unseen, but that the two of us make a trip there to meet everyone, see the church, and talk about the possibilities. They would send us our plane tickets. We agreed to do that.

Nenita had never been to Cheboygan before, and the least we could do was take a look, they said. But I already knew the tactics of the people, and I had no qualms about what they intended to do. They wanted to convince us, once we were there, to make the move. In March of 1981, the two of us flew to Cheboygan, Michigan, to visit Huron Street Tabernacle.

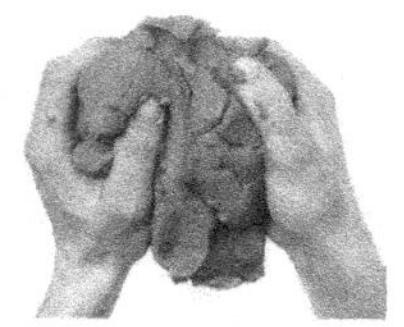

36

It had been snowing that day, and by the time we arrived, the snow was already quite deep. Nenita had never seen anything like that before, and she was fascinated by the sight that greeted us as we landed. She had seen a little snow in North Carolina, but nothing like this. She was intrigued by how it clung to the trees and the wires and how it covered the houses.

"Isn't it beautiful?" I said.

"Yes," Nenita agreed. "Take a picture. Come on, take a picture of it." She was as excited as a little child.

As soon as she could, she ran out of the airport to put her hands in the snow and see what it felt like. The people who had come to meet us had no problem seeing that it was her first time to see a serious snow.

We stayed with one of the elders of the church and his wife. That night, after they had gone up to their bedroom (and we had gone to the room they had assigned to us downstairs), Nenita was so excited that she couldn't think about going to sleep. She stood at the window for the longest time watching those big flakes drifting down from the sky.

She was there so long that I finally said, "Well, come on then," pointing to the door leading from our bedroom directly to the outside. "It's the middle of the night, but if you want to see the snow, we can."

"I do," she answered. "I want to feel it some more." Eventually we did get to sleep that night.

On Tuesday evening, we had dinner with the chairman of the board at his house, and then we all went to the church. There, the entire leadership of the church was assembled to meet us, including all the Sunday school teachers. They all acted as if it our coming was already a "done deal," that we were already their pastors.

"Give us some time," I said. "We came to get the feel of things."

That night Nenita said to me, "You know, this *is* a wonderful place." I didn't say much, but I could sense that God was working.

Wednesday night would be my first time to preach at the church on this occasion. That morning, a group of the men and women of the church picked us up and took us out for breakfast. We were in another house for dinner, and some of the church people joined us. The people kept saying things like, "We're praying. We really believe that you are the man for this job."

When they said these things, Nenita would look at me and say something like, "Well, the Lord needs to speak to our hearts too."

"We're not here as a candidate," I told the people. "You just invited us over for a visit," but in my heart, I was already saying, "Lord, if this is Your will, I'm ready to accept it."

In the end, we had to put a fleece before the Lord. If one hundred percent of the people voted to make us their pastors, we would accept, but surely that was impossible. We would not accept a two-thirds majority or any other less than perfect vote. It had to be all or nothing, and everyone knows that such a vote happens very rarely.

Wednesday night came, and it was snowing so hard that we wondered if anyone would attend the service. But everyone did.

I had already noticed a change in Nenita's tone. It was nothing I had done. I had tried everything in my power to convince her in the past weeks that we should do this, and nothing had worked. But now the Lord was doing it.

After I had ministered that night, the chairman of the board got up and announced, "Now, we would like to ask all of our visitors, all those who are not members of the church, to make their way out into the foyer. We would also like for Pastor Ray and his wife to go out while we have our business meeting."

Three people who were not members stood and made their way out into the foyer, and we went with them. But something didn't feel right. We knew that they were surely discussing us in there, and it didn't seem right to be excluded. "If they're talking about us in there," I said, "it's unfair that we cannot be present," and we went to the door and asked to be admitted to the meeting. We were given permission, and we made our way back inside and sat down.

They surely were talking about us. Each member stood and told his or her viewpoint, why he felt that we should be their pastors, what he had dreamed or what vision he had seen. As each one lent his or her confirmation, the excitement rose.

"We've had no pastor now for a whole year," one man said. "And Pastor Ray is a man of God. We really believe that." And others spoke in a similar fashion.

Eventually, I raised my hand. "Listen," I said. "I'm really happy about all the things you have said here tonight. Thank you. But I need to hear from God. I need to be sure that what you are proposing is of the Lord. And I'm not yet sure.

"One of the reasons I am hesitant to immediately accept your offer is that I would not want to limit you. We speak English, but it's not English English. It is Filipino English, and it's very different from what you speak."

"But we have no problem understanding you," someone said, and everyone agreed, and that ended that argument.

My hand went up again. "But we're Filipinos, and this is a totally Caucasian church and community." There were only two other foreigners in the room that night. One was a Chinese doctor from Taiwan, and the other was a Filipina married to an American serviceman. Later, one black lady would come from outside of the community to attend the church, but there were no blacks in the congregation that night. Surely this argument would sway them, I thought.

Then the wife of a prosperous businessman stood up and said, "If the problem is the color of our skin, we can paint our skin brown if you want, and we can order palm trees flown up from Florida. We'll plant them in front of the church to remind you everyday of the Philippines."

Tears sprang to her eyes as she continued, "But you must stay because we have no pastor. We need you. The Lord spoke to us and showed us that you are the man to lead us."

Right about then, I felt like melting into the woodwork. What more could I say?

Then Nenita stood up. She said, "You have known my husband for a while now, but he has come to visit you only for a few days or a week or two at a time. You really don't know him all that well. How can you be so sure that he is the right pastor for you?"

"We don't need to know him," someone said. "We can easily see that he is a man of God."

The discussion seemed to be at an end, and the chairman said, "Now, Brother and Sister Llarena, could you please excuse yourselves, and we will continue our business meeting." And we went out.

The other three people, an elderly couple and a young lady who were not members, were still waiting in the foyer. "How do you feel about all this?" I asked them.

"Well, since we're not yet members of the church, we have no official right to say," they answered, "but we would really be happy if you would become the new pastor." They had known me from other visits. "We have been praying that the Lord would speak to your heart."

"Well, keep praying," I said. "I'm certainly not closing the door. I just want to be sure this is the will of God."

Then suddenly we heard clapping and shouting and stomping. The older lady turned to me and said, "I guess you're in, Pastor."

Someone came and asked if we would come back into the meeting. The chairman turned to us. "Pastor," he said, "we want you to know that we voted on you being our new pastor, and it carried unanimously, one hundred percent. Every single member of the church voted to receive you as our new pastor." There had been no opposition whatsoever, no nays at all, and that is what I had asked the Lord to do as a confirmation.

For some reason, I was still hesitant to fully commit to them. "Well, I'm not going to say no, but I'm also not going to say yes right now," I told them. "The Lord needs to speak to my heart. You need to pray, and I need to pray."

The wife of the chairman, who was also the church pianist, spoke up and said, "How long does it take to hear from God?"

"Well, it depends," I answered her. "Sometimes it takes a day, sometimes it takes only a minute, but sometimes it can take a whole year. God can do it quickly if He so chooses." The meeting ended, and we all went to a restaurant for some refreshments.

Another round of meals was planned for the next day. We would all have breakfast together. Then the men would take me out for lunch, while Nenita would fellowship with the women in a church luncheon. "What is this?" I asked. "It almost feels like an official reception."

"No, no," someone offered. "This is just our plan for meals tomorrow."

We would be going back home to San Francisco on Saturday so that we could be in the church on Sunday.

That night Nenita and I lay down to sleep. After a while, she thought I was already asleep, and I thought she was already asleep, but we were both wide awake. She shook me. "Wake up!" she said.

"How are you feeling about all of this?" I asked.

"How about you?" she said. "How do you feel?"

I was more concerned about her. I had already been thinking that we would go back to San Francisco, take some weeks to put things in order, and then, in a month or so, accept the generous offer to move to Cheboygan.

"God spoke to my heart that this is His plan," Nenita said.

"What about the snow?" I queried.

"I love it," she said.

"What about the cold?" I asked.

"I think I can take the cold," she said. I agreed. I would need a good overcoat, but I could survive.

"The church people are so nice," Nenita said, "and the whole community seems to be so friendly."

And then there was the matter of the parsonage. It was a lovely house, and the people had told us that it could be ours if we wanted to live there. In the meantime, the secretary of the church was living in the house to keep it open. They gave us the option of buying the house or having the church buy it for us.

We had refused, up to that moment, to discuss salary because we didn't want money to affect our decision. If it was God's will for us to be there, the salary would be right.

Midnight came and went, and we were still talking about what we were feeling.

"Oh, look how bright the moon is," Nenita said. "She had never seen the moon reflected off of the snow like that. "How gorgeous!"

I was thinking to myself, She has always hated snow before, even when it was just a little. She always hated the idea of living where there was a lot of it. Then she was saying something else: "I wonder what kind of schools they have here." I heard her, but my mind was elsewhere, and I wasn't responding. Surely this must be a sign from the Lord.

"Honey," she continued, "before we go home, we need to find out what kind of schools they have here. We need to consider the children."

"Okay," I responded. "We'll look around tomorrow and see some of the schools." Now we were suddenly talking as if we were ready to move.

"Well," I finally said, "we'd better get some sleep or we won't feel like doing anything tomorrow." It was already two o'clock in the morning, so we stopped talking and went to sleep. But we both dreamed of moving to Cheboygan, and we both woke up convinced that such a move would be of the Lord.

We were both very excited the next morning, but we decided to move cautiously. "Let's not say anything to anybody," I told Nenita. "We'll just let things fall into place smoothly as the Lord directs."

At breakfast that morning, one of the church leaders didn't waste any time asking, "Did you hear from God yet?"

"Well," I said, "we're still praying."

"Well, could you please ask the Lord to hurry and show you what He has already shown all of us?" They were already making many plans because they were so sure in their hearts that we were the pastors they had been looking for.

After breakfast, they drove us around to see the city. At some point, Nenita said, "How about the schools? You know, the junior high, the high school? Joy would be beginning sixth grade that fall so they showed us the junior high. We also saw the high school and several elementary schools. By then, it was time for lunch.

As we dropped Nenita at the church, we stopped to visit with some of the ladies. Before leaving them, I had opportunity to whisper to Nenita, "Let's not say anything yet." She nodded her agreement. It didn't take us both long to break that agreement. Each of us, in separate places, at the same time, "spilled the beans."

The men asked me what I was feeling, and I felt I could no longer keep my feelings from them. "But," I added, "that is just my feeling. I need to talk to my wife."

Nenita did exactly the same thing. She told the ladies how she was feeling. "But that is just what I'm feeling," she told the excited women. "I need to talk to my husband."

After lunch, we went back by the church to pick up Nenita. The men noticed that the women were excited, and the women noticed that the men were excited. I turned to Nenita. "What did you say?" I asked her.

"What did you say?" she asked me, smiling broadly. And there, in the presence of all the members of that church, the thing was sealed. The glory of the Lord came down upon us in that moment and made us to know that we had reached a correct decision. Within moments, we and everyone else in that place were weeping.

The news spread like wildfire over the town. That night, there was a potluck dinner at the church, and it was unusually well attended. "When will you be coming?" people were asking excitedly. It was a time of great celebration.

The next day someone took us to see the parsonage. If we didn't like it, they told us, they were ready to help us find a house we did like. As it turned out, we didn't like the parsonage. It was situated on a noisy, busy road. It would be a dangerous place for the children to play. So, we went from house to house the rest of the day looking for something more suitable. How we would pay for it was not an issue. "We will make the payments," the chairman of the board told me, "but it will be your house."

I didn't want to live far from the church, and, although they showed us some beautiful lake-front homes outside of the city limits, I was afraid that travel back and forth in winter might be too difficult for us. I also wanted to live where Nenita could easily walk to the grocery store if she needed to when I was out of town.

Again, the next day, two men, the chairman of the board and another good brother, helped us look at homes. When we had seen many and none of them seemed suitable, someone said, "Maybe we should just rent something to give you more time to get to know the area and to decide just where you prefer to live."

There was one more house for us to look at. It was a five-bedroom Colonial just two blocks away from the church. The owner was from California. Her husband had died suddenly of a heart attack, and she was moving back to Los Angeles. "If you like the house," the men told us, "it will be available by the time you get back. In the meantime, we can clean and paint it and do anything else that needs to be done."

"Let's go and see it," we said, hoping that this last house might be something we both liked. It was beautiful, and it had four bedrooms and a bath upstairs and a wonderful living room, family room, and kitchen downstairs. There were lovely yards in both back and front. All of this just two blocks from the church.

"This is ideal," I said. And the men asked the owner how much she was asking.

"$55,000," was the answer. We had already been told to sign for any house we liked, so there was not much more to discuss. We did take a little time to think it over, but we bought the house.

Many of the people came out to see us off on Saturday. We needed to be back in San Francisco for the Sunday services.

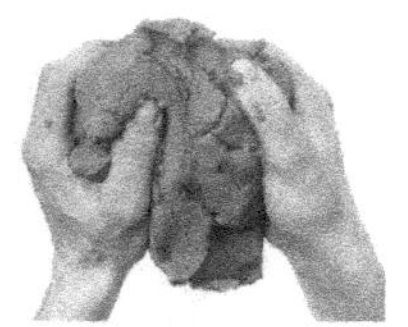

37

We had told Pastor Stewart that we were going to visit the church in Michigan, and while we were away, he had sensed that something serious was up and had been praying, "Lord, please don't send Pastor Ray away from here. But whatever Your will is, I'll be happy with it." When we got back, he asked, "How did things go?"

"Well," I said, "we have decided that it is the will of the Lord for us to go there. I promised that I would be there by Palm Sunday for the Palm Sunday and Easter Sunday services, and then I'll come back and we'll pack to move. I still have a speaking engagement to fulfill in Reading, California, as well."

We not only needed to get ready to move; we also needed to find someone to rent our house. As it turned out, those two needs were answered in one family. After we got back and our decision to move began to become known, a family came along quickly and said they wanted to rent our place. They were also willing to help us pack up all of our things to facilitate the move. God knows how to answer prayer.

I flew to Cheboygan for Easter week, and when I left there someone handed me some money. It was, they said, for my airline ticket and for my moving expenses, enough to rent a U-Haul truck and pay the gasoline for the whole trip. "And," I was told, "we want to go ahead and pay you your first two weeks' salary." I had not known until then what my salary would be. I had accepted the job without knowing. Now, I realized that it was to be generous.

Nenita and our friends were busy packing while I was away. I wondered how we would get everything across the country. Michigan suddenly seemed like a very long way. As it turned out, a friend who had moved to San Francisco from New Jersey told me that he would be willing to drive the U-Haul for us. "Then you and your family can all fly out," he said. "Let David go with me." They would take their time, he said, and would need at least a week to go the distance. After we had our suitcases packed, he told us to go ahead and he would get some men from the church to load everything else.

We called Cheboygan and told the church people when we would be arriving. We were amazed to find almost the entire congregation at the airport to greet us. Seeing the crowd, others thought that some dignitaries had arrived. There were bouquets of flowers for my wife and mother and the girls, and everyone was crying and embracing us.

As we pulled out of the airport, there was a long caravan of vans and cars. "We will go straight to your house," we were told. "It has been cleaned and painted." The only problem was that we had no furniture. We had told the church leaders that we would be shipping our furniture, but that we had no good beds. They said they would buy us some beds, so when we arrived at the house, there were only two pieces of furniture.

There was food already cooked and waiting for us, but the whole group wanted to go to a restaurant, so that food could wait until later. Then, for a while, we were invited to eat in a different house every evening. Someone came each morning and brought us breakfast. If we didn't want to go out for lunch, someone would bring it to the house.

It was nearly a week and a half before the truck arrived, but we were already settling into our new work. I was in the office every day and loving it, and Nenita was working to decorate the house to her tastes. "When the truck arrives," we had been told, "call one of us, and we'll all be here to help you unload. Don't try to unpack all that by yourselves." And that's exactly what happened. The day the truck arrived, almost the whole congregation came to help. As you can imagine, the unloading went very fast.

We began our pastorate at Huron Street Tabernacle in Cheboygan in April of 1981.

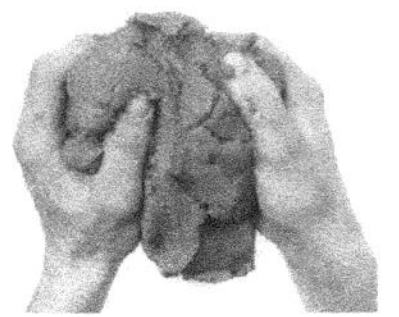

38

We were very happy in Cheboygan until, toward the end of 1983, the Lord began moving upon my heart in another strange way. I felt Him saying, "It's time to fold up your tent, pack up your suitcase, and go back to your Canaan Land." I understood Him to mean that we should return to the Philippines.

At first, this thought seemed to me to have come from the devil himself. The church was doing so well that we were about to buy thirty acres of land to build a new sanctuary. Surely this was not the time to leave that place.

Before we had arrived there, what had been built for an overflow area for the sanctuary had not been used for quite some time and had been turned into Sunday school space. After we were there just a year, we had grown sufficiently that we had to reopen that overflow area and use it in every service. God was pouring out His Spirit in the area, upon Lutherans and Catholics and Wesleyans, and many of these people were looking to us for spiritual growth and sustenance. It was a very exciting time.

Still, for some months I had been feeling strangely restless. Something was exciting my soul, something I could not really put my finger on at the moment. I was still enjoying my preaching and ministry, and people were being blessed, but for some odd reason, I was beginning to feel like a fish out of water. I actually felt like I was being suffocated at times.

I began to pray about this matter, "Lord, is this a signal or a sign from You that my time here is up? I love it so much here that this is where I would like to retire." Nenita and I had even been looking at properties for sale beside a lake, thinking that we would like to build ourselves a cabin where we could live after retirement. When the church leaders heard about it, they were delighted and said they would build the cabin for us. We had it made in Cheboygan.

So, why was I feeling so restless? Nenita was so very satisfied where we were that I had not yet dared to tell her anything about what I was feeling.

In July of 1983, we made a trip to the Philippines. I was invited to speak at a Missions Conference in Cebu, where there was an Assembly of God Bible College. We stayed there for a week, and it was during this time that God began to make His plan more clear to my heart. "You need to come home to your land," He said to me. "You have traveled around the world, and now it's time to pay tribute to your own country."

For the time being, I kept this to myself, although I did say to the Lord, "Okay, Lord, but You will need to make this thing clear and cause it to happen."

In the natural, I did not really want to go back. We had too many things going for us in our adopted country. We were very well known and respected in the Cheboygan community. Even the mayor had become a friend, and I could feel free to go to his house. Other prominent people loved and appreciated us, especially a local judge, and we felt a spirit of togetherness in the community. It was a wonderful place to live and a wonderful place to raise our children. It was the American dream come true.

After we had gotten back to Cheboygan and I looked around at all that we had there, I again felt that the words that had come to me must be from the devil. He was trying to get my mind off of what I was supposed to be doing at the moment, so I kept going, kept moving forward in my ministry there.

Then Harold McDougal called me and invited me to Maryland and West Virginia for a little celebration of the twentieth anniversary in their work in missions. One service was to be held in Hagerstown, Maryland for their friends and family there, and another service to be held in his hometown, Fairmont, West Virginia, for their friends and family there. He wanted me to speak at both events.

I was thrilled. "Sure," I said, "I'll come." The meetings were to be held in January.

It was a very cold January when Harold met me at the Baltimore/Washington Airport. He had been taking trips back to the Philippines every year and sometime twice a year, and we had many things to get caught up on. We knew many of the same people and the same places. I was anxious to hear what he had been experiencing, and he was anxious to hear what I had been experiencing.

As he told me about the great things he had been seeing in the Philippines and shared with me his vision for the future of that country, for the first time, I began to open up about what I had been sensing but denying.

On our drive from the airport to his home, we took a wrong turn and the trip doubled in time. Then the drive to Fairmont took several hours there and several hours back, and all of this time we were able to share together what was on our hearts.

In Fairmont, we stayed in his parents' home. Aside from the anniversary banquet, there was another important event on the schedule. Harold had an appointment to be interviewed on a popular morning television program by Jack Kincaid, the manager of the Christian television station in Clarksburg, West Virginia. He wasn't sure that Jack would have time to work me in, but he said he was going to suggest it and see what happened.

Jack and I liked each other from the start, and he arranged to work me into the final segment of the program that day. The Lord was at work in all of this.

I had become so convinced of the will of God by this time that I mentioned on the program that God was sending me back to my homeland after eleven years of living in the United States. As we parted, Jack said to me, "Let's stay in touch, and when you're ready to go back, I would like you to come again, and we'll see what we can do to help you."

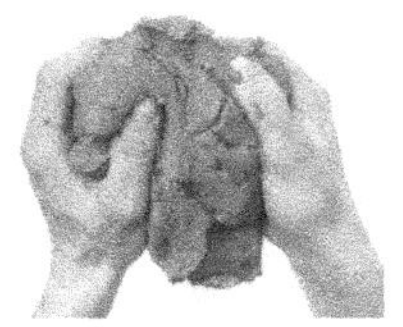

39

As soon as possible after I got back home to Michigan, I began to tell Nenita what was happening. Her response was firm. "No way," she said, and war broke out.

"I'm not going back to the Philippines. I'm not that stupid. If God is calling you to go, then you go. God is not calling me, so let me stay here with the kids. You go there, and I'll stay here. I'll even get a job to support the family, and I can also send you some offerings." She was dead serious, and she went so far as to say that she would send me money once a year for airfare so that I could come and visit the children.

"And don't try to force me to go," she warned. "If you try to force me, I'll file for divorce." And she meant it.

"I'm not kidding," she assured me. "I love you, but I'm not going back to the Philippines. No way! That's final."

"When you resign from the church, I'll continue paying the mortgage on this house. You won't need to support us. I'll send you money every month."

Of course, I could not entertain any of these thoughts for even a moment. "No," I calmly answered. "Wherever I go, you need to go. I'm still the head of the household, and wherever the head will go, the body must follow."

"Oh, yeah?" she challenged. "Just try me!" And for the moment, the discussion had reached an impasse.

Joy was already in junior high, and David was twelve, so they both had strong opinions, and Nenita proceeded to get them and

Leah to take her side. She reminded them of the mosquitoes in the Philippines, and Joy and David agreed that when they had gone in 1980, the mosquitoes had indeed been bothersome.

"The smell is terrible there," the kids now chimed in, "and we couldn't find any American food there at all."

"And the houses are not like here. Most of them don't have a decent shower, and none of them have bathtubs. Really, Daddy, taking a bath with a pail of water is terrible. And we wouldn't have any friends over there."

Well, Nenita seemed to have won that skirmish. The kids were convinced that the Philippines was a terrible place to live, and I was standing alone in my desire to return there. It was four against one.

From then on, when we were eating together or when we were sitting together in the living room, I would say something about getting ready for our move to the Philippines, and immediately the rest of the family would jump up and run out of the room, leaving me alone with my thoughts.

This war went on for two and a half months, until Nenita was sleeping with Leah. She would no longer sleep in the same bed with me.

My mother was living with us through all of this, and I confided in her my dilemma. To her, an old-fashioned Filipina mother, this was scandalous. "Why don't you ask her for a divorce?" she suggested, outraged.

"Mom," I answered, "God is not in the business of dividing families. They just need to recognize that He has set me as head of the household. Sure, God hasn't spoken to Nenita; He speaks to the head of the family, and the members of the body should follow. Sooner or later they will recognize that."

"God didn't speak to my heart," Nenita would insist. "I'm not stopping you, Honey. You go. But if you try to force me, the papers will be filed." I didn't know what else to do but to pray.

Prior to going to speak at the Thanksgiving services in Maryland and West Virginia, I had been on the verge of trying to work out a deal with God. "It seems impossible for me to go," I had told Him. "I'll go once a year and do a crusade, but I don't want to live there again."

One day I was flat on my face on the floor of the sanctuary, praying about this matter. "God, I will double my mission offering to the Philippines. Just don't send me back there. I will go once a year and will sponsor a crusade. I will minister myself, but I don't want to go there to live."

I tried to think of my children in those circumstances, and I couldn't bear it. "Lord, no," I said to Him.

Then God spoke to my heart and said, "If you obey Me and follow Me, I will show you My strength and My power, and I will prosper you. But if you do not obey Me, your ministry is over. I will leave you." The words were a little different than the ones He had spoken to me in Guam so many years before, but the message was the same.

"I would rather die than have You leave me, Lord," I prayed, and my decision was made. Just to be sure that this was the will of God, I asked the Lord to give me some sort of confirmation through another person. That's when I had been invited to West Virginia, and the call was confirmed through the McDougal family. My heart was settled, but that didn't prevent war from erupting in our home.

I told the leaders of the church what I was feeling, and sometimes one of them would ask us, "When are you guys planning to go?"

Invariably, Nenita would answer, "He's going, but we're not."

Soon, my members were commenting, "We sense some hostility here."

"Well, he's the only one who wants to go," Nenita said, defending her position. "The rest of us don't want to go. I don't want to go, and my children don't want to go. The Lord has not spoken to my heart, so I'm not going. He can go. It's okay with us."

"Oh, Pastor Ray," some of my best members were saying to me, "you'd better think twice about this. You certainly don't want to end up in divorce court."

I really didn't know what to answer. "God has spoken to my heart," I said. "He will honor my decision."

In private I spoke candidly with my children. Joy especially was old enough to understand. "You are my children, and you need to listen to what I feel as your father."

"Dad, if you force me," Joy responded, "I'm going to run away from home." The principal had gotten wind of this family disagreement and had told Joy that if we left, she could stay with his family and finish her schooling. I understood what she was feeling. She was in the band, and she had made many good friends, but principle was principle, and God had spoken.

One day the assistant principal told Joy that she was also welcome to stay with his family, but that she should never run away from home. "There is no way I'm going to leave any of you here," I finally said to Nenita. "Over my dead body."

"Well, then, if you insist on forcing me to go," she warned very seriously, "then this is the end of the marriage."

What should I do? What *could* I do? As I pondered what I should say or do, the Lord spoke to me and told me to just leave Nenita and the children in His hands for the moment and to concentrate on getting myself ready to go. That wasn't an easy thing to do, but I set about to do it.

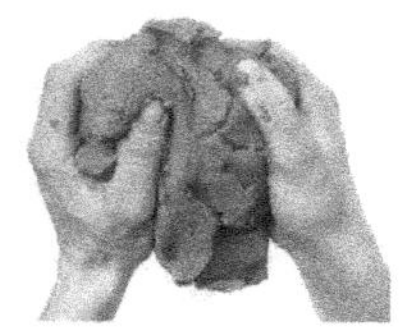

40

I officially resigned from my position in the church and started packing my things at the office. I had many books there and many personal belongings.

A friend of ours worked at Proctor and Gamble, and he was able to get me some large used boxes from their plant. Slowly, I added box to box, until the stack of things began to mount in the garage.

I hadn't told this friend what I was doing with the boxes, and when he saw it, he said, "Oh, you're getting ready for your trip."

"Just him, not us," Nenita chimed in.

Some of the church people tried to reason with her. "Don't you think you're being awfully stubborn."

"No," she boldly responded. "I'm not being stubborn. The Lord has not spoken to my heart. God has not called me, so I'm not going. He says God has called him, so he can go. I'm not stopping him."

"But you're married to him," they insisted. "The two of you are one flesh."

"No, this calling is just for him," she fired back.

There was still time. It was May and I was not planning to leave until July, so I continued to pastor the church, and I continued to seek God concerning my family.

I sent a letter to the Philippines telling our friends and family we were coming, and then I called. "We're coming home," I said.

"The whole family?" I was asked.

"Yes," I answered by faith. "We're going to start a ministry there."

The husband of my niece was a pastor, and I asked the two of them to join us in this new venture. "Pray about it," I told my niece.

"Well, we already have a commitment here, but we'll see what develops when you get here," she answered. I asked her to inform some key people that I would be coming.

Toward the end of May, we had a visiting missionary family come by. They had been stationed in the Philippines some years before, but now they were working in Africa. One day, as we were all finishing up a meal together at the table, the man asked, "How long have you been here now, Pastor Ray?"

I said, "A little over three years, but now the Lord is sending us back to the Philippines." Nenita's face turned red, but she didn't say anything.

"We'll be praying for you," the man said. "It will be a difficult adjustment, especially for your children. The lifestyle there is so different. Let's pray together right now." We prayed, and they said they would be remembering us in prayer. I thanked them profusely.

The following week, the leaders of the young people of the church decided that instead of having their regular Friday night meeting at the church, they would all go bowling together on Saturday night. One of the youth advisors, a lady, advised me of their decision. She said they would like to take Joy and that they would have her home at a suitable time. I told them that was fine as long as she was not home too late because the next day was Sunday.

I was studying in the living room later that night when I heard Joy come bursting through the door. The lady who had taken her was at the door, asking permission to come in. Joy had been crying so profusely, she explained to me later, that she was afraid something was wrong with her and had insisted on bringing her home.

"Dad, where are you?" Joy called.

"I'm here in the living room," I said. "What's the matter? Why are you crying."

"I thought something happened," she responded. "I'm sorry, Dad. I'm really, really sorry. I'm just so stubborn. I know this has been really hard on you."

I sat her down and got her a glass of water. Then I said, "Tell me what happened."

"I was there in the middle of the bowling alley," she said, "with the ball in my hand, and I was about to throw it, when the Lord spoke to me and said, 'You're being very silly. And you're not being rebellious to your dad; you're being rebellious to Me. You're not fighting your father; you're fighting Me. By sending your father home alone, you are not cooperating with My will."

Frightened, she had dropped the bowling ball and run out of the place. The lady advisor, seeing what had happened, ran after her and asked what was wrong. "I'm going home," was all that Joy had said.

"But it's quite far," the lady had insisted. "Can't you tell me what's the matter?"

But Joy didn't know how to explain it. She said, "I just want to go home." They had jumped into the lady's car, and she had brought her home.

"Dad," Joy said to me, "I'm going."

Nenita was upstairs, but she overheard this conversation. She came down, but she didn't say much at the time. After the lady advisor had left, Nenita said, "Well, then you and your daddy can go," and she was very upset by this turn of events.

"But, Mommy," Joy told her, "the Lord spoke to my heart. This is of the Lord." Nenita didn't answer.

I was very happy that we were making progress. Joy's enthusiasm caught on with David and, because the two of them were excited, Leah got excited about going too. They all began to make their plans.

I wondered how this would affect Nenita. "Well, okay," she said to the children. "The three of you go with your dad; I'll stay here."

"Okay," the kids answered, and returned to sorting their toys and deciding what they wanted to leave behind.

I rejoiced because I could see that Nenita was having to seriously consider her position. I wondered if this was the time for me to speak to her, but the Lord said to me, "Don't say anything. Just bite your tongue. Leave it to me."

I continued my packing and my plans for the Philippines. I called a shipping company to get an estimate on how much it would cost to ship all of our household goods. "I'm going to ship everything," I told them. They told me about the advantage of using a container. The cost of sending a twenty-foot container from Michigan all the way to the Philippines was only $1,500 and a forty-foot container only $3,000. I was amazed, and we rented one of each. I decided that whatever would not fit inside the containers, I would send to California to be stored in our house there.

The man who drove the U-Haul to Michigan had moved into a small apartment in the downstairs of our house in San Francisco and was doing the maintenance, collecting the rent from the upstairs, and making sure the apartment was rented. I called him and told him our plans. "We'll be flying to California from here and then on to the Philippines. Could you come here and take the rest of our belongings to San Francisco?" He agreed. He and David would pack the truck and drive it across country.

Still, Nenita had not agreed to go. She was very angry, and she kept insisting, "If you force me, that's the end of it. You can have the children. They want to go with you, so you can have them."

Periodically, she asked the children, "Who would you like to go with, your daddy or me?" and now the answer didn't vary: "Daddy."

"Fine," she said.

Although I had cleared out the office and packed everything for shipment, one Friday night I was at the church studying and praying about who would take over the church. I was confident that the Lord would send the right person.

I went home quite late that night, somewhere around eleven thirty, and everyone was already in bed. Nenita was sound asleep, so I entered the bedroom very quietly so as not to wake her up. I carefully got into the bed, and I fell asleep.

I had been asleep just a couple of hours when I was awakened by the movement of the bed and Nenita's crying. I thought she must have been having a nightmare, so I attempted to wake her up. But she was already awake.

She threw her arms around me and said, "I'm going! I'm going! I'm going!"

"Where are you going?" I asked. "It's two o'clock in the morning."

She began to explain through her sobs. The Lord had spoken to her in a dream and told her that if she didn't go with me, she would regret it the rest of her life. She was ready to go.

After telling me this, Nenita could not sleep, and she got up and put on her robe. "Well, let's go down to the living room," I said. "We'd better start listing down all the things we need to take."

"I want my washing machine," she said, "and I want my dryer." Then, "I want my microwave. I want everything. I want all of the furniture."

I said, "Honey, anything you want to take with you, that's fine with me. And if there is something you want to take that we don't have yet, we'll go out and buy it." Eventually, we went back to bed, but we woke up early the next morning. We had a lot to do.

In a great rush of excitement, we drove all over town, getting old newspapers from all of our friends to use to wrap our dishes and other delicate things.

Nenita said to the children, "Sort all of your things," and they did. Within two weeks time, the entire household was packed and ready to move. When women put their mind to it, they can accomplish amazing things.

The next problem was getting everything into the forty-foot container. Nenita wanted to take our water bed. She wanted all of the beds, in fact. She wanted to take everything. She didn't want to leave anything behind.

Antiques had been cheap in Michigan, we had bought quite a few, and she wanted to take them all. "But the container is only so big," I told her. Not everything will fit into it. We could have a garage sale for some things, and other things that we want to keep we can send to California."

"We'll have to rent another container, then," she said.

"We can't pay that much to ship old furniture," I suggested.

We had a china cupboard that was built in 1878. It had belonged to a pastor by the name of Reverend Schulyz. We sent that to California, along with other old pieces.

In short order, everything was ready to go.

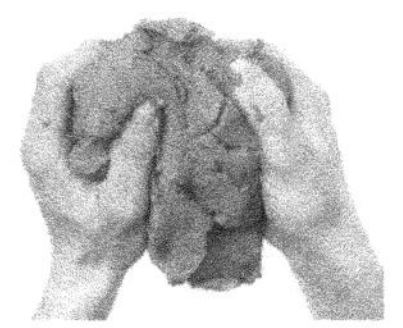

41

In the meantime I applied for missionary status with the Assembly of God church, and the churches of our district became very excited about the prospect of having a missionary from our area. All of the necessary forms were sent to headquarters, but when the answer came back, it was not good. "We cannot endorse Reverend Llarena as a missionary," the letter said, "because he is going back to his own country. Our policy is that anyone returning to his own country cannot have a missionary appointment. If he chose to go to some other country, it might be different."

The district officers called to tell me how sorry they were. They had been excited about the prospect, but the policy prevented it. They gave me the name of the man who had issued the statement and his phone number in case I had any questions for him. I did. I called him and asked him to explain the decision to me.

"We're not questioning your ability," the man told me. "But this is our policy."

"But this is a ridiculous policy," I protested.

"But it's there," he answered, "and we need to honor it."

When I got that news, it seemed to me like a terrible blow, almost as if my whole world had collapsed. I had been counting on that support. But when I prayed about it, the Lord said, "They're not the ones sending you. I'm the one sending you. So, what's your problem?"

A former drug addict from West Virginia had come and preached for us in 1982. While he was there, he said, "We would love to have you come to West Virginia. We could book you into different churches there to speak." I thought of him now and called him. "I'm going to start itinerating a little," I told him. "Can you help me?"

"Absolutely," he responded, and he booked me for a month of meetings in different churches.

I called Jack Kincaid and told him I would be coming to the area. "Good," he said. "Come and stay with us, and we can do some television programs."

Soon after I arrived in West Virginia, I began to share with Jack what had happened. "I'm not even endorsed by my own organization," I lamented. "Their churches may not be open to me, and any money they give me may not be counted toward their total missionary giving. What can I do?"

"Well, some of my friends are connected to other churches," he said. "I'll see if they would like to have you." And he kept me busy over the coming months. I occasionally went home, only to come back again to continue itinerating.

During this time, Jack said to me, "If you are still lacking anything, I'll help you." On one of the programs we were doing one morning, he announced: "Pastor Ray will be going back to his country. Because of that, he cannot be endorsed by his own organization. It's against their policy. But he is stepping out in faith anyway, so we need to remember him in prayer. Anybody who would like to help him, you can send your donation here to the station, and he will get it."

Day after day, I spoke on those morning programs, and they were recorded so that when I was out preaching somewhere else, he could replay them. Very quickly, I became known in a wide area of West Virginia. Before I left the station that first time, Jack said to me, "I pledge five thousand dollars right now. Let me know when you're ready to go, and I'll send it to you."

The people of Clarksburg, Valley Head, Elkins, Grafton, Wheeling, Job and many other towns in West Virginia were very generous with me and kept me busy until the end of June, and a number of churches made a commitment to send us some monthly support. Four of those churches were to be very faithful to us during our coming missionary years.

While I was preaching a few nights of revival meeting in my first visit to a church in Canaan Valley, West Virginia, a Mennonite couple attended. They invited me, along with the pastor of the Pentecostal church where I was preaching, over for dinner. The next time I went to that town, they wanted me to stay with them. I asked the pastor what he thought, and he agreed. In time, this family, the Millers, fell in love with me and treated me like the son they had lost, driving me anywhere I wanted to go and doing many wonderful things for me. It was like that in many West Virginia towns.

The Millers' son had wanted to be a missionary but had become ill and died. They asked many questions about our move to the Philippines, about what we were taking and how we were taking it. I told them about the containers. "Good furniture is very expensive in our country," I explained to them. "We will be shipping most everything we need. My wife wants to take her microwave and her washer and dryer."

"How much is that going to cost?" they asked.

I told them, and they replied that they wanted to pay it all themselves. They also put money in my hand the day I left and told me they would be supporting us monthly. I loved visiting the Millers, who have now gone on to their reward. They were just like my own family.

I'm not sure how we would have survived on the mission field without the generous support of the churches of West Virginia. Of course, God always has His way of supplying our needs. His way, this time, was through these wonderful people. I found it very interesting that Harold McDougal had come out to the Philippines from West Virginia, he had inspired us, and now the West Virginians were supporting us. I find this remarkable because West Virginia is not counted among the wealthy states, but it has its rewards awaiting in Heaven. How great are the ways of the Lord!

Jack Kincaid and the people Channel 46 also continued to help us from time to time, and every time I made a trip to the States, he invited me to speak on his programs.

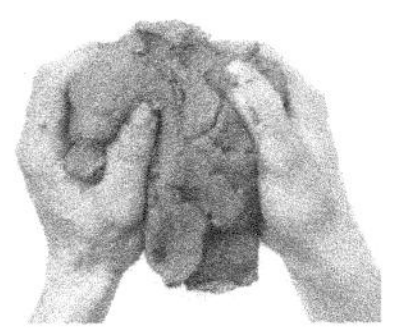

42

In 1974, during the time that I was still going back and forth to Michigan to conduct revival meetings, the friend who had been the best man at my wedding, a doctor, had migrated from the Philippines to Chicago. He came through San Francisco, and we touched base again after many years and began corresponding. I called him one day to say that I was on my way to Michigan and that my flight would pass through Chicago. "I would like to see you," I told him.

"Good," he said. "Why don't you come early and spend the night, and we'll take you out to see the city."

During that visit, my friend took me to visit Faith Tabernacle, a great church in the heart of the city of Chicago. Henry Carlson, the lay-preacher, was the founder and pastor. Pastor Carlson told me, "I'm glad you came. We have a special guest speaker tonight." That was my introduction to Faith Tabernacle. Every time I would go to Michigan after that, I would stop by Chicago.

Toward the middle of 1975, Pastor Al Smith took over the church. We had known each other for so many years that I now had a closer link to the church, and I visited Chicago more often. When I was pastoring in Michigan, I often went to Chicago to preach.

Now, when it was time for me to go back to the Philippines, the people of Faith Tabernacle also pledged to support me. In fact, they said, they wanted to be the sending agency, and they provided me all the documents I needed to present to the Philippine government. They also shipped things for us and helped us with special offerings.

The last time I had been in Clarksburg with Jack Kincaid, I had been on my way to Chicago. Jack handed me an envelope that day and said, "I'm sorry, Ray. It's not as much as I had hoped for."

"Well," I said, "every penny counts. Thank you."

"When I opened the envelope, it contained five thousand dollars."

There were six of us traveling: Nenita and myself, the three children, and my mother. And when we arrived, we would need a place to stay, money to begin the ministry, and a little cushion against hard times. I needed to raise a little more to cover everything.

When we were in San Francisco, Pastor Stewart asked me to preach, and the church gave us a good offering. Friends we had written to all over the country did their part too. Churches where I had preached in Hawaii also sent offerings. Before we knew it, we had enough, and we scheduled our flight.

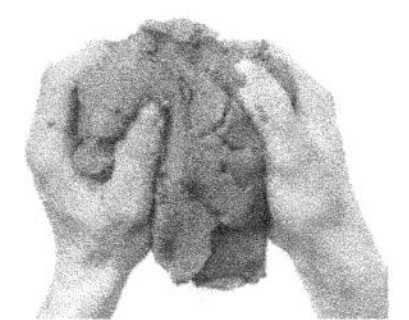

43

We were on our way to the Philippines — excited, rejoicing, happy, and ready to venture into a new ministry. What was awaiting us we did not know. What the future held we could not say. All we knew was that God was leading us.

Personally, I was in "seventh heaven." I had always found it to be challenging and thrilling to follow the Lord one step at a time. He had never failed to surprise us. This would be no exception, I was sure.

We landed in Manila on July 8. All of my brothers and sisters, nephew and nieces were there to meet us and some of our Christian friends as well. It was very moving.

We checked into a local hotel that night and stayed there for a week as we searched for a suitable place for our family to stay. It was not easy to find such a place, and eventually we moved to my sister's place for a few days more. Then, an elderly lady who had a large house but was occupying only one room of it, agreed to rent the rest of the house to us. That was the place where we started our ministry, with twenty-five people in our living room for the first service.

We began immediately forming a new corporation to facilitate our ministry, and we began having services. I was also invited to speak in some other churches.

The fire that had been sparked in the early 1970s, especially among Catholics, had not died. It had spread, and many Catholics were forming into Charismatic groups. I was invited to speak to many of these groups. Services were held each day at noontime in the lobby of City Hall in Quezon City. I spoke there.

When people heard me preach, they asked, "Where's your church?"

"We don't have a church yet," I told them, "but we will, and we'll announce the opening." We didn't take this step for several months. In the meantime, we kept meeting in our house with those we considered would form the leadership of our new group. We prepared all the paperwork, but we didn't have money to file it at the moment.

Nenita and the children went with me wherever I went. We not only preached in churches; we preached to groups of people gathered outdoors, under mango trees, in open fields, in auditoriums and public and private halls. We were constantly on the go. It was wonderful!

In each place, we told people that we had come to start a new ministry. "Let us know when you get started," some would say. "We will attend."

I said, "There will be an announcement in the paper and on radio and television when we start."

Our problem was that we could not find a locale that we could afford. Everything was too expensive. We searched and searched, but nothing surfaced.

Then it came to the point that we knew it was time to start the church. People were being saved as we witnessed on the street, and we had no place to take them. For the time being, we sent them to other churches, but that didn't seem to be a suitable long-term solution.

Two of my nephews were in the ministry, working with the Baptist Church, and were conducting prayer meetings in their house in Marikina. They said to me, "Uncle Ray, when you are ready to start your ministry, we will help you." Their mother, who had not been a very strong Christian when I left the country, got very excited about this prospect.

When we finally got started, they brought fifteen of their young people from Marikina to join us. We had an instant young people's group. It is amazing how God organizes these things!

Some of my friends had been attending another church and were not happy there. They had not been able to get actively involved in the church, so they decided to join us too. We knew that we could have fifty to sixty people at least in our early services, so we had to find a place that would accommodate a good number.

We eventually rented a building belonging to the Department of Education. We had enough to rent the place for a Sunday morning service lasting three hours each week. We had no musical instruments and no sound equipment, so we had to buy a guitar, a drum set and a sound system. There was a piano in the place, and that was a blessing. We set the opening meeting dates for Faith Tabernacle of Asia.

We put up banners across the nearby streets, we printed and distributed fliers, and we had the meetings announced on radio. We sent people to advise the television stations about our new venture, hoping to get some free ads. CBN especially gave us some free spot announcements. We named the church and told the location. Two or three times we were on television, and we all went to the streets with the fliers.

Our opening Sunday finally dawned. That morning, I said to Nenita, "I'll be happy if there are just twenty-five people there. I'm not expecting a particular number. God knows what He wants to do." We went to the place an hour ahead of time to prepare it for the first service.

We would be very limited by the circumstances of the hall. We would have to set up everything and then remove everything when the service was over. We put the banners up on the wall, and then we had to take them back down again. We had no place for Sunday school, so we would only have the main service to begin with.

At nine thirty, only two other people had arrived. At nine forty-five, two more came. By ten o'clock, a few more people had already come, and we decided to start our service. Then the miracle happened. Within ten minutes after we had started, the hall was suddenly filled with people — more than two hundred of them. Wow! What excitement! It was powerful! I cried.

"After the service that morning," I told the people, "we will have a leadership meeting with prayer."

One lady pastor stayed that day and in the leadership service, she said to me, "I want to join you. If you don't mind, I could handle your Sunday school and young people's program."

I said, "That's wonderful, but I don't have much to pay you."

"You won't need to pay me to begin with," she answered. "My husband is working. Just give me an offering."

Under the leadership of that lady pastor, the youth activities took off from the word go, with the young people coming from Marikina. Because my nephews had commitments, they could not break those immediately. I told them to take their time.

We started with that, and then God started to bless, and we grew. Sunday nights and Wednesday nights people would come to our house, but it was already very crowded. I went back to the officials in charge of the building and asked them if we might also be able to rent the place on Wednesday nights. They agreed.

It quickly become apparent to me that we needed an office near the church. We lived rather far away, and people needed somewhere to come during the day for prayer and counseling. There was a large house, a mansion really, directly across the street from that building. It also belonged to the Department of Education, and it had been empty for a very long time. I asked if they would be willing to rent it to us, and they agreed to rent it for fifteen thousand pesos (US $300) a month. We had no money, but we said we would take it. It was in that building that we developed our Sunday school for children, the children's church, and our Wednesday night and Sunday night services. Not only were we saving money; but now we had an office.

During the daytime, the young people and the praise and worship team were practicing their songs. In the afternoon they would go out and witness in the parks. It was powerful. It was not difficult at all to start the ministry. We stepped into something that was already boiling, something that was already on fire. By the time of our first anniversary, we were running eight hundred to a thousand people in our Sunday services.

We were only in that place for a year. There we celebrated our first anniversary. My nephew joined with us, and the lady pastor trained the young people and the Sunday school teachers. I was able to concentrate on training leaders for the church.

In July of 1985, a year after the church was born, we were conducing our first campmeeting for young people, and there were some eighty young people in attendance. "We will have this once a year," I told the people, "because this is the way the ministry will grow."

We didn't send any of our people to other Bible schools. We trained them ourselves, and soon they were teaching Sunday school, doing visitation work and jail and hospital ministry.

Each Sunday, we carried all of our equipment into and out of the large auditorium, but now at least we didn't have to take it home. We just stored it across the street in the other building we were renting. That was much easier.

Then we were able to make an even better arrangement with the caretaker of the building. He would let us in on Saturday night to set everything up so that we didn't need to be so rushed on Sunday morning.

God was also beginning to bless us financially. The people were growing in their faith, and their giving also increased. We would need that increase. God had some big steps of faith for us to take.

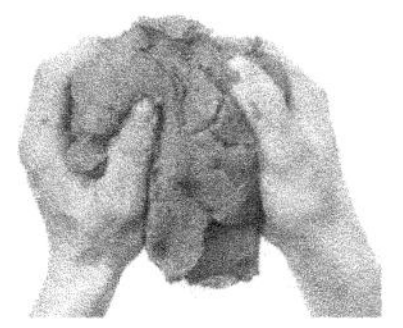

44

THIS HALL WE HAD BEEN RENTING WAS ON THE THIRD FLOOR, AND there was no elevator in the building, so over time, some of the older members began to complain that it was too difficult for them to climb the stairs. We had begun to pray and ask the Lord to help us find a better place, to open the door for us to have our service in a more accessible location. Soon after that we met Ramon Rosa, owner of the Broadway Centrum Shopping Mall. He had an auditorium there that had been rented by a pastor for a church service, but the group had recently canceled their lease and left.

Brother Rosa attended out first-year anniversary celebration. Later that day he said to me, "I would like to offer our auditorium to you for the church. It would be less rent than you are paying here, and you could use it as many times each week as you want." It didn't take us long to decide to accept his offer, and we moved our services into the Broadway Centrum Auditorium. Everyone agreed that it was a wonderful location.

There were many stores in the mall, and often shoppers who were there for one reason or another would hear our singing and step inside the auditorium. When they did, we invited them to come to know Jesus. Some shoppers forgot what they had come to the mall for and got interested in the Lord and His work instead.

The mall was well air-conditioned, and because it was hot outside, many people came into the mall just to get out of the heat for a while. When they heard us singing, "so lively and happy," they came inside. The end result was that many were saved.

Despite the size of the place, we had to have two services each Sunday morning and one in the evening to get everyone in. God was moving in our midst, and we were being blessed and multiplied.

After we moved into that new space, one day Brother Rosa said to me, "I have some vacant offices that you could rent."

"We couldn't afford to rent them all," I told him. "Just rent us one space for now." But he gave us such a good price that we rented the entire area. Now, we had a fellowship hall, offices, and classrooms.

In the middle of 1985, when I came back from two weeks of ministry in India with Pastor Kurien Thomas, Nenita said to me, "The church is growing so fast that we are going to need to have more musical equipment." In short order, God had sent us such an influx of musicians that we now had a full orchestra. We had clarinets, flutes, saxophones, trumpets, and trombones. The leader of the orchestra was a graduate of the University of the Philippines School of Music, and he also directed the choir. With these two impressive musical groups, we launched out into evangelistic meetings all over the city of Metro Manila. This, in turn, spurred even more growth in the church.

45

One of the ministry goals Nenita and I laid out when it became clear that we were indeed returning to the Philippines was to start an orphanage. We felt that God had put that burden on our hearts. Up to this time, however, we hadn't had funds to undertake such a project, and we didn't have a suitable space to use for that purpose either. So, we had pushed that project into the corner of our minds. But we had not forgotten it; we were praying that the Lord would show us when and how to begin.

Not long after I came back from that trip to India, we received a phone call one afternoon advising us that a neighbor lady who already had several children and was not married was trying to sell her latest child. She was asking only two hundred pesos (equivalent to about US $4.00) from anyone willing to take the child. I couldn't believe what I was hearing. I went right over to see what was happening.

I found the child to be only five weeks old, and he was a beautiful boy. "Why are you selling this baby?" I asked the lady.

She said, "I cannot afford to take care of him."

"Well, I'll gladly give you two hundred pesos to help you out," I said, "but surely you'll want to keep your baby. I would gladly take him, but he's your baby."

"No," she said, "I don't want another baby. I can't care for another baby." And I could see that she was under a heavy strain.

I took the child home. It had been a long time since we had a baby in our house, and we had no diapers or bottles or blankets.

We would need a bottle sterilizer. Nenita said, "Stop by a drugstore and pick up a few things." I did, and we were instant parents again.

We named the child Philip Andrew. He slept with us, and Nenita felt that he was the beginning of our dream to have an orphanage. Our children were also very excited to have a baby in the house, and they loved to help care for their new brother.

A year before this, using the young adults of the church, we had developed another new ministry that we called The Midnight Express. Late at night these young people would go out and begin to witness to those who were living and sleeping on the streets. Sometimes they also gave these people food or other help, and they always invited them to church.

One particular night, the young people came upon a man in the Camal area of the city who had a little boy with him. Both the man and the child were little more than skin and bones, for they were suffering from malnutrition and tuberculosis. The man told our people that he had lost his job. Then the family had been put out of their apartment. His wife had left him, and he and his two children were left to fend for themselves on the street. One child had died, and now the second one was near death. "Could you help my son so that he will not die?" he pleaded.

"We'll do what we can," the young people answered, and they set out for our house.

At five o'clock that morning, a knock came at our gate. "Pastor! Pastor! Emergency! Emergency!" someone was calling.

I wondered what kind of emergency could be happening at five o'clock in the morning. I went out to open the gate, and the young people told me about the man and particularly about the boy. "If we don't do something for him," they said, "he will die."

When I asked Nenita what we should do, she said, "They should bring him here."

"They're in Camal," the young people said, "but we can go back and get them."

"Yes," she said, "go back and get the child, but we must also do something for the father."

"Let's do this," I suggested. "Divide into two groups. One group can bring the child back here, and the other group can take the father to the hospital." I told them what hospital was receiving TB patients and told them how to get there.

When we saw the child, we were amazed. He was three years old, but he could not stand, and he could not talk. There was the smell of death upon him. We gave him a bath and dressed him.

He would not eat anything, and he said nothing to us. His eyes were yellow, and his belly was distended. It was apparent that he was dying. We decided to take him to a hospital too. It was clear that he needed immediate medical attention.

At the hospital, the admitting officials wanted to know where the parents of the child were. "We don't know the parents," I told them. "The father is also sick, and we had him taken to another hospital for treatment. They have been living on the street."

"Well, we cannot accept this child," we were told. "He is indigent."

"But I'm bringing him here, and I'll be responsible for him," I insisted.

"It doesn't matter," they said. "You're not the father."

"Listen," I said, "are we going to stand here arguing while this child dies?" The staff member we were talking to went off to find someone of higher rank who could possibly make an exception.

Finally, the director of the hospital came. He said, "We are not equipped to handle this situation. You must go to Children's Hospital."

We accepted that verdict, but when we arrived at Children's Hospital, we were told exactly the same thing. The fact was that we didn't even know the child's name, and we didn't know his parents' names. I said, "You have to understand. Some of our people found this child living on the street in Camal. I am Pastor Ray Llarena. We want to help this child to survive. We must help him. So, I will be responsible for whatever expenses are incurred in his treatment. I will pay for his medications and his doctors' bills."

Eventually it became necessary for me to raise my voice a little so that our case would not be pushed aside. I said, "Listen, I brought this child here. That was my responsibility. Now, if he dies, that's your responsibility, and you will answer for it."

Again the director was called for, and we waited until he arrived. When I explained to him the case, he said, "Okay, if you are willing to sign that you will be responsible for all of the medical bills, I can do it." I signed.

All of this was extremely traumatic for the child, who would start crying and not stop. A doctor was finally able to examine him, but his verdict was not good: "This child is very sick. He has a fever. If he survives the first forty-eight hours, then there may be hope for him, but I doubt very much that he will survive."

We had to send someone to the other hospital where the father was being treated to get the child's vital statistics. He said that the child's name was Christopher and that he was three years old. I stayed with Christopher the rest of that day, a Friday, and all day Saturday. The child sensed that I loved him, and he clung to me, crying when I had to finally tear myself away, and the nurses would have a hard time calming him afterward.

On Sunday morning, I told our people about Christopher and told them that he might die if God didn't do a miracle. "Let's all stand up and join in prayer for him." And we did, we really prayed, with faith that God would work for Christopher. I cried like he was my own child.

After we had prayed, I told the people how I had signed the hospital papers by faith that we could somehow take care of the resulting medical expenses. That morning money was given to pay the bill. By now, we had business people in our church and others who had inherited wealth, and they gave freely for this cause.

After the service, Nenita took the children home, and I ran to the hospital. The news from the doctor was both good and bad. "Amazingly, he has survived the first forty-eight hours," he said, "but unless he starts eating, I don't see how he can survive much longer." Three years old, Christopher weighed a little less than eleven pounds, and he still looked like death warmed over.

"Here is the list of medicines you will need to buy," the doctor said. I took it and ran to the drugstore and bought the medicine. When that was done, I said to the doctor and nurses, "I need to go home and get some rest," but when I tried to go, Christopher cried terribly, so I went back into the room and stayed.

"His TB is very serious," I was told now. "It will take time for him to heal. He will be here for months." We knew that such a treatment would cost an exorbitant amount, so we prayed seriously, and Christopher was released after only three weeks in the hospital. He had quickly begun to mend, and his spirit was greatly improved. He was happy. The father also recovered and was released.

When we took Christopher home from the hospital, we suddenly had two small children in the house. "Honey," Nenita said, "I think the orphanage has been born."

We took the children to church with us, and we began announcing the fact that God had placed on our hearts before leaving the U.S. that one of our ministries in the Philippines would be an orphanage and another would be a Christian school. "It seems that the orphanage is being born right now," I said. "We must pray to know the complete will of God in this matter."

The children took a lot of our time, so we asked for volunteers who would come and help care for them a few hours at a time so that Nenita could have time for other things. Others would come so that she could go shopping or just go outside and enjoy some time alone. The people who were helping us in this way got very excited about it, and prayers began going up for the proposed orphanage.

People began to say to me, "Is it okay if we look for a place to have that orphanage?"

"Well," I said, "It's okay to look, but don't get too serious because we don't yet have any money to rent a place."

The general expenses of the church were pretty well taken care of by this time. The congregation had grown sufficiently in size, spiritual maturity, and financial blessing that we were no longer being stretched. The church was not paying me a salary because we depended upon our own support from America, but that didn't always arrive on time or with guaranteed regularity, and I wondered if, at some moment, we would need to ask the church to help us. Could we afford to start an orphanage?

A few weeks after Christopher came home, one of the ladies of the church came to visit us. She told us about a woman in her neighborhood who had many children. Some of the children had gone to the province to be distributed among relatives, but one of the boys was put into a Catholic orphanage called the White Cross Orphanage.

This child was known to be quite unruly, and sometimes he bit or punched some of the other children. He created such a confusion in the place that the Catholic sisters who ran the home decided to send him back to his mother. She, however, had no way of supporting him, so it was a dilemma. "She's asking if you would be interested in taking him in," the woman said. "His name is Elvis."

I asked Nenita what she thought, and she said, "Bring him."

Elvis was a definite problem. He was about four years old, but he would urinate against the wall or standing on top of a table. When he went to the bathroom, he would play in his own waste. He would kick the other children.

Nenita said to me, "This child has demons inside of him. This is not normal." It was true. Sometimes we had to hold him down, and still he would scratch, pinch, bite, or kick us and even spit on us.

At the church one day, I said to the congregation, "There's a spirit in this child that is clearly not of God. It's a filthy, dirty spirit, and it's creating a lot of chaos in our home. Let's pray." We prayed, and from that day forward, Elvis became a normal child.

Now we had three orphans. Elvis was light-complexioned and good looking, Christopher was a sensitive and gentle child, and the baby, Philip Andrew, was growing quickly. It was all exciting to watch. We just added another crib, and we were doing fine.

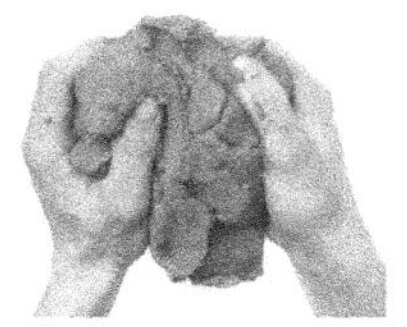

46

Toward the end of October of 1985, a set of twins were brought to us, and we now had five orphans. Then three more came, and we had eight. At that point, I said, "We need to start looking for a place now, Honey. This is becoming too much." We asked the congregation to pray and start looking in earnest for a good location for the orphanage.

We met a Christian lady whose family business had failed, and she and her family were planning to leave for the United States. They wanted very badly to sell their property, but no one was buying. The economy was not good, and the political situation in the country was tenuous. Students were demonstrating against the long-standing president, Ferdinand Marcos, wanting him to step down, and the country was preparing for an election scheduled for the following February.

The house this family was leaving was ideal for our use. It was situated in what is known as the Blue Ridge, a section just on the outskirts of the capital overlooking the valley and the town of Marikina. It had a large enclosed compound with a high fence around it and a strong gate. It would serve our purposes well, so I offered to rent it. We came to an agreement and rented the place.

The next problem we had was who was going to manage the orphanage. Nenita loved the children so much that she wanted to do it herself. "We can go back and forth," she said, and that was feasible because it was only a five- to seven-minute walk from our house to the orphanage.

Our children were very excited about having the orphanage so close. "After school," they said, "we can just take our homework with us and go over there and play with the kids and help out wherever we are needed."

Next, we would need more than volunteer help in such an undertaking. We needed some qualified professionals, particularly a licensed social worker. We began to search for such a person.

We needed to buy some cribs and some beds, and many other things that would be needed in the daily life of such a large home. We set this need before the Lord in prayer.

One day, after the home had been open just two weeks, Mrs. Rosa, the wife of the man who owned the mall, asked if she could visit the children. When she arrived there, she had candies for everyone. And before she left that day, she placed a wonderful offering into our hands. It was a check for nineteen thousand pesos. In this way, we were able to buy everything we needed.

After applying for a license from the Department of Social Welfare to operate the orphanage, we learned that the requirements were very strict. We needed to come into compliance quickly or the government threatened to take the children from us. The processing of those papers proved to be so complicated that we had to hire a social worker just to complete it. For a country that was so poor and so in need of this type of help, the requirements seemed almost ridiculous to us, but what could we do?

Every now and then, we received an offering at the church to help us with something we were doing in the home. Eventually we had to establish a way that people could give regularly because suddenly we were swamped with children. They were coming from every direction.

Twins came from a tribal group in Palawan. It had long been the custom among the tribal people in our country that if twins were born, one of them must have an evil spirit. Often both of the children would be killed because no one could be sure which one had the evil spirit. A pastor in Palawan had heard that these particular twins were about to be killed and he suggested that they be given to the orphanage in Manila. When I heard about this case, I took one of the social workers and flew to Palawan to receive the children.

The wife of a Filipino pastor died, and afterward the pastor found that he could not cope with raising his children alone. There were no other family members to care for them, so he asked us if we would take them. I went to receive these four children.

A twelve-year-old was found roaming the streets by The Midnight Express ministry and brought to us. In a matter of a few months, we had nearly thirty children to care for. We had begun with very young children, but now we had children of every age, and some of them required schooling. What now?

47

By New Years of 1986, the Philippines was totally absorbed in the famous People's Power Revolution. The results of the election went against President Marcos, but he refused to recognize the voice of the people and lift his order of martial law. Huge crowds of people now took to the streets in protest. One day I called Brother and Sister Miller in West Virginia, and they said, "Son, we saw the news about the revolution. Get out of there while you can still get out."

I said, "I don't think we can. It would cost us five thousand dollars just for our air tickets."

"We'll send you the money," they said. "Just get out of there quickly. Bring all your children and move quickly. We see things getting worse quickly." They sent us the money, but by the time it arrived, the airport had been shut down, and no flights were going in or out.

To avoid danger, we just stayed close to home and didn't go into the downtown areas where the demonstrations were taking place. The carnage was terrible. People were being shot by the military, mowed down as they demonstrated peacefully. The only thing we could do was pray.

Gradually, a wonderful thing began to happen. People were taking to the streets, not with guns, but with prayers. They were facing down tanks with flowers and smiles. It was phenomenal, and it gained worldwide media attention.

This powerful movement that came to be known as the People's Power Revolution convinced the Marcoses that they must leave the country, and Mrs. Cory Aquino, wife of assassinated Presidential Candidate, Benigno Aquino, took power. Things quickly quieted down and became peaceful, and the airport reopened.

Now, we were free to leave, but suddenly there seemed to be no reason for us to go. I called the Millers again and told them that we would not be traveling so we would be returning their money.

"When are you planning to come to the States next?" they asked.

"Maybe in May," I told them. "We've been here two years now, and it would be nice for us all to have a visit home."

"Then just keep the money," they graciously replied. "You'll need it then." That's what we did.

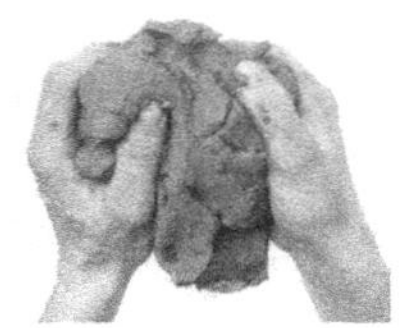

48

THAT SPRING WE WERE TRYING TO DECIDE WHERE TO ENROLL OUR orphans for the coming school year. I hated to see them attending public schools because it seemed possible that they would quickly lose many of the good teachings we were endeavoring to give them. "We need to find a Christian school, but one that will enroll them free of charge," I concluded. "Otherwise, it will take a huge amount of money for their schooling."

"Nobody will do that for all seven or eight of them that need it," Nenita replied. And we began to pray seriously about this situation.

One day our lady youth pastor said to me, "Pastor, we could start a Christian school for the orphanage and use the Accelerated Christian Education, or ACE, curriculum. We can use the rooms of the office building as our classrooms, and the playground can be outside in the yard of the house." This idea seemed to me to be so wonderful that we all began to pray about it.

We had six rooms and a hall, and it was large enough to gather everyone. Although we had no money to undertake such a project, we decided to start, believing God to supply as we went forward.

We would have to recruit some teachers and send them to a church in Cavite City to be trained, and we would be expected to pay for that training. We also needed classroom chairs, blackboards, a place for the children to eat, separate bathrooms for boys and girls, and other things that would cost us a considerable amount. Nenita felt confident that God would provide for all of these improvements. I wrote some letters to friends in America, hoping that they would want to help us.

When the church people heard about our plans, they said they also wanted to send their children to the school. Then Christians from other churches in the area contacted us and said that they, too, hoped to send their children. This was suddenly becoming a very big project. By the time classes opened, we already had eighty-nine students.

All of our teachers were serving on an offering basis, and what we were able to give them made their work a sacrifice, but they were willing to do that, accepting this work as their mission for Christ. Another long-held vision, this one for a Christian school, was coming to fruition.

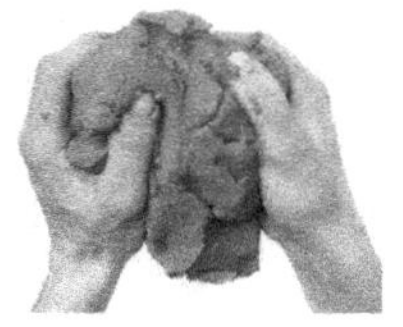

49

Just at the time we were getting ready for the opening of the school in June of 1986, I had some speaking engagements in the States — in California, West Virginia, Michigan, and Chicago. I had told Nenita that we would need to leave toward the end of April to be back there in time, but she felt that both of us should not leave at once at such an important time.

Also our children were attending Faith Academy, and the school year at Faith was different. Our children had not yet finished their studies for the year. "Maybe you should go ahead of us," Nenita suggested. "The children and I can follow later, after they have finished." This seemed like the proper thing to do, so I went ahead and had my first meeting in Chicago.

Toward the end of that meeting, Nenita called to say that she needed more time to get things ready for the opening of school. She had decided to send the children ahead of her by themselves, and she would follow. She had been able to borrow some money locally to do the needed work, and we promised to repay the money when we returned from this trip to the American churches.

The children arrived in Chicago the second week of May and Nenita had tentatively committed to joining us the last week of that month. She wanted to be sure to be with me when I went to Michigan. Then she called to say that she was delayed longer and would join us in West Virginia. The alterations on the building were costing more than we had anticipated, and she was still lacking a few teachers. We went on to Michigan, hoping that when we got back to Chicago, Nenita would be there.

It would be the first time for my family to accompany me to West Virginia. Jack Kincaid was very excited about our coming and had gotten other pastors prepared to receive us for meetings. We were all looking forward to our days there.

Then, just as we were finishing up our time in Michigan, an important phone call came for me from friends in Chicago. "You need to go home immediately," they told me. "Your sister called to say that your wife has been rushed to the hospital, and she is in critical condition and may need surgery."

"Is this some sort of joke?" I asked.

"I'm sorry, but it's not," I was told. "Here's the number of the doctor attending her. You can call him." And they gave me the number.

I called the doctor. He said, "Reverend Llarena, I am sorry to tell you that your wife is in very serious condition. She has an aneurysm, a rupture of a blood vessel in her brain. She is still hemorrhaging, and this could be life-threatening. She is already paralyzed on one side of her body, and we need to do surgery to release the pressure of this bleeding and to stop it if we can, or she could die."

Immediately I thought of the pressure that had been on Nenita with the orphanage and the school. She had been so faithful to carry this burden, and I prayed that God would spare her life.

We quickly excused ourselves from Michigan, flew back to Chicago on the first available flight, and made immediately arrangements to return to the Philippines. It was a eighteen-hour flight with a stopover in Honolulu. We arrived there on June 10 and went straight from the airport to the hospital.

Nenita could communicate with us, but her speech was slurred by the paralysis she had suffered on that one side. She wept as she saw the deep sadness her affliction caused the children. They cried so and she cried so that I eventually asked someone to take them home. Her health was so delicate that she didn't need this further distraction.

The people of the church prayed with us, and Nenita was able to regain her speech. She told me what had happened. She felt so pressured by the upcoming opening of the school year. It was already the first week of June, and the facilities were not yet ready. The greatest pressure was having to borrow the money to finish the work, and those who had agreed to loan the money had some sort of delay. Then, on top of all that, she learned that my aunt had died.

She rushed to the home to see my cousins, and she remembered it being very hot that day. From there, she went right to the church for the Wednesday night service, but by this time she had a terrible headache. She collapsed there in the church that night and was rushed to the hospital, already partially paralyzed.

"I'm going to get out of here," she told me, "because we have so much work to do yet with the church, the orphanage, and the school."

"Well, don't you worry about any of that now," I told her. "You just concentrate on getting well. Everything else will be fine." Classes had already begun, and I told her how well they were all doing.

Then Nenita's doctor came to me and said, "I need you to sign this consent form. Nenita needs emergency surgery. I won't lie to you. Her chances of survival are about fifty-fifty at this point.

We cannot guarantee that she will survive the surgery." By faith I signed the consent form so that the hospital staff could begin prepping Nenita for surgery.

In the end, the surgery did not take place that day. After further consultation, the doctors decided that they needed to take two weeks and "condition" my wife for the surgery. Toward the end of the June she would undergo the procedure. I practically lived there in the hospital over the coming weeks.

Then, the day arrived. That morning, just before they wheeled her away to the operating room, Nenita squeezed my hand and said something that shook me to the core, "Take care of yourself," she said, "and don't let anything happen to the orphanage. I know that there is still a lot of work that needs to be done for the school, but God has been good to you, and He will help you now."

What was she saying? Why was she speaking like this?

When she continued, my questions were answered: "I don't think I'll be coming out of this."

"No," I said, "don't talk like that. God will bring you through it. You'll see." And she was rushed away to the operating room.

The surgery went on for more than eight hours, and as I sat in the waiting room with some of my other family members, many thoughts assailed me. I hadn't liked what Nenita had said to me just before going into the operating room. She hadn't been positive at all. I was believing God for a miracle. We must believe. He had never failed us, and He could not fail us now.

Eventually, one of my family members said to me, "This may take longer than expected. One doctor said it might be up to ten hours. I think you should go home and clean up and get some rest. Then you can come back, and by then maybe the surgery will be over."

I went home, took a shower, tried to rest for a couple of hours, and then I went back to the hospital. The surgery was still in progress.

When it was time for the children to come home from school, I asked my sister to go fix them something to eat and to stay with them. "If they would like to come here for a couple of hours later, you could bring them," I told her.

Finally, a doctor came out to say that the surgery was finished and had gone reasonably well. Nenita had survived and was in the recovery room. It would take her a while to wake up, but he felt like they had done a good job and that she would recover with time. They had taken a vein from another part of her body and had grafted it into her brain to seal the ruptured area.

By the middle of that night, they had brought Nenita back to her room. She was still sedated. The doctor warned me, "It is very crucial that your wife not get excited until her rupture is healed. She cannot be aggravated or upset by anything. Any kind of excitement or strong emotion could cause this repair to be damaged. I don't want her to have any visitors at all. Your children will be allowed only to look at her for short periods of time through the window. They cannot go into the room."

Some of our church people and other pastors came by regularly in the days ahead to pray for Nenita and to stand with me in that dark moment of my life. They tried every way they could to relieve me.

The hospital gave me a room on the fifth floor where I could rest at night, and during those most critical days, the children stayed there with me. They would sometime go home and eat and bathe, but then they would come back and sleep at the hospital. Each night they brought their school clothes, changed in the morning in the small bathroom in the hospital room, ate their breakfast in the hospital cafeteria, and Nenita's nephew would then drive them to school.

Within a week, Nenita seemed to be responding well. Her vital signs were good, I was told. "In a few more days, we will remove the bandages," her doctor said. "You will need to get her some sunglasses, so that the sunlight will not be too bright for her. Any wrong signal or emotion, any shock to her system — whether it be happiness, excitement, or sadness — could trigger a devastating reaction. We will need to condition her little by little back to natural responses. But she seems to be doing fine now. I think she will recover fully."

With that news, we had a little celebration there in the hospital and had special food brought in for the doctors and nurses. God was good. He had heard our prayers.

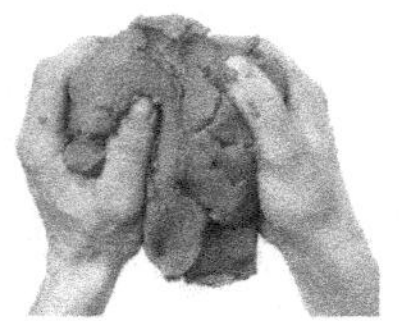

50

The doctor had also recommended that I hire a nurse to give Nenita the special around-the-clock care she required. "She will have a nurse here in the hospital assigned to her at all times," he said, "but that nurse will have other patients to attend to as well. It would be good if you could find someone with special experience to deal with this situation. Nenita needs constant attention."

I wondered how we could afford this expense, but in a phone conversation, the Millers assured me that they would send money to cover any such added expenses. "Get her the help she needs," they told me, "and we'll take care of the bills." So we did.

Early on the morning of July 6, the special nurse came to say that Nenita had spent a very restless night and that she had somehow developed a temperature. We all understood that this was not good. We called the doctor and he came and examined Nenita.

"This may very well indicate that she has some infection," he said, and he called for a specialist in that field to deal with the situation.

Nenita received special medications to deal with the infection, but through the next day she remained restless and feverish. That night her fever went even higher, and her blood pressure began to alternately rise and fall. The medical staff found these developments to be very alarming.

Then the nurse noticed that Nenita's stomach was very hard and that she was moaning. She quickly reviewed the charts and came to the conclusion that Nenita had become constipated. Some of the medications she had been taking had hardened her stool, and no one had noticed it until then. Nenita had not been able to properly discharge her waste for nearly a week.

The nurse tried giving Nenita a suppository, and when that didn't work, she called the doctor and told him what was happening. He suggested that they try some manual form of extraction. "But be careful," he told her. "Do it very slowly. Don't agitate her."

This was done and seemed to help somewhat, for Nenita began regaining consciousness, but she still could not talk. (I later wondered why they had not immediately given her an enema.) Her lips were distended, her eyes were bulging, and she had an animal-like look to her face. Alarmed, the nurse called the intern, and then several other doctors were called in. When they had examined Nenita, they said to me, "This situation is really not good. Your wife's blood pressure is rising and falling dangerously. She is in a very delicate condition. She may not make it."

At midnight, Nenita's blood pressure dropped precipitously, and nothing the medical staff could do would bring it back up. They came to the conclusion that her repaired vein had ruptured again. She was again hemorrhaging internally. She was transferred to a more secure room and put on a breathing apparatus.

By the time all of this was accomplished, it was morning. I told the children that their mother was not doing well and that they should stay with me that day. My sister came with some of her children and was there to comfort me in that darkest of hours.

That morning Nenita died. I might have been totally devastated by this, for God had answered my prayer so many times, and it was difficult to know why this case was different, but He had warned me of what was to come. Two nights before Nenita died I had been praying in the hospital chapel and God had said to my heart, "It's time for her to go home." This had been difficult for me to accept. I was still believing and trusting Him for a miracle, and the people of the church were fasting and praying and believing that she would fully recover. How could we let her go now? But the Lord knew best. If He had said it was time for her to go home, then surely I must accept His will.

Later Joy told me that God had spoken to her about the same time he spoke to me. He had told her, "I'm taking your mother home. You'll have to help your dad now, and you must be a mother to your two siblings." She had not told me this because she didn't want me to worry. I had not told anyone what the Lord had shown me either, hoping against hope that I was wrong.

When the doctors advised us that Nenita was clinically dead and that it was only the breathing machine that was making her lungs move now, Joy told me what she had felt, and I told her what I had felt. "Let's surrender her to the Lord," we agreed. We did that together. Then Joy began singing the song "In His Time," and we all joined in.

After that we sang another song and another. Some of our church people had gotten the news by then, and they had come to comfort us. Now they joined us in singing. There was such a beautiful presence of the Lord in that room that the doctors and nurses were crying too.

Eventually we joined together and sang "To God Be the Glory," and as we sang that great chorus one final time, Nenita took her last breath and stepped over onto the other side. It was about ten o'clock in the morning, and I was suddenly desperately alone.

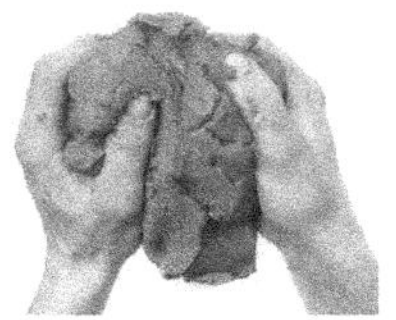

51

It took several hours to finish all of the paperwork, and afterward the body was placed in the hospital morgue. It could not be released until all of the hospital bills were paid, I was told. That was hospital policy, and there seemed to be nothing I could do about it. I certainly didn't have that much money at the moment.

I asked my sister to take our car and take the children home. I needed to figure out how I would pay the hospital bill, and then I needed to make some arrangements for the funeral. I would take a taxi, I told her.

Several of the nurses in that hospital were members of our church, and they eventually convinced the billing office to receive a promissory note for the balance of the hospital bills, so that I could go and make funeral arrangements. By now, it was already four or five o'clock in the afternoon.

"Can you recommend to me some funeral home?" I asked one of the hospital staff members.

"We have a list of funeral homes that are connected to the hospital," I was told. "You could just start calling them and see what they say."

None of the homes I called could give me a price before I went to their location to choose a coffin. In time, I realized that I could not make these arrangements by phone, and I walked out the door of the hospital.

Outside the hospital, a huge thunderstorm had struck. Rain had been coming down in torrents as only it can in the tropics, and the streets of the capital were flooded. Somehow this storm seemed to be symbolic of what was happening in my own life. There had been many tears throughout Nenita's ordeal, but that was nothing compared to the torrent that now came. My beloved Nenita was gone, and I was alone with my three children.

There seemed to be no taxis available at the moment, so I walked in the rain, and I cried. I screamed, as the torrents soaked my clothing and the sadness of utter loss gripped my soul. I walked and walked and walked, until I eventually reached a funeral home near Camp Cramey, some twelve to fourteen kilometers (about eight and a half miles) away.

I looked at the available caskets and quickly came to the conclusion that I couldn't afford any of them. I called my sister to ask how the children were doing. She said they were crying and had refused to eat. I talked to them and encouraged them to eat something. "I'll be home in a little while," I said. "I'm trying to make arrangements for Mommy's funeral."

I so much wanted to be with my children in that moment, not out there roaming the streets, trying to find a suitable casket for my wife. "I think I will call the church," I said to my sister, "and see if there is anyone there with a car who could come and help me?"

"Stay right there," she said. "I'm sending the car." And she sent my nephew to drive me wherever I needed to go.

Some of my nieces came too, and together we went to another funeral home. I liked a casket I saw there, and the owner, a Christian believer, agreed to give me a considerable discount so that I could afford it. It was beautiful.

The man had seen how I was suffering through all of this and was very sympathetic. "I don't have the money with me," I told him, "but

I will have it for you by tomorrow. But in the meantime, I would like for you to have the body picked up from the hospital morgue. I'll go home and change and bring back some of Nenita's clothes, so you can dress her. Could you bring her body to the church tomorrow?"

He agreed to do that. It was already seven or eight o'clock in the evening. "If we can pick up the body right now," he told me, "we could even deliver it to the church tonight."

"Whatever you can do," I told him, "I will greatly appreciate it."

I went home and changed clothes. I tried to eat, but I found that I couldn't.

The children said to me, "We want to go with you."

The rain had stopped for a while, but the water was still high in the streets.

We gave the funeral home time to get the body, clean it up, and do the embalming. By ten thirty that night we were back at the home to see Nenita's body. The staff at the funeral home had done a wonderful job. Nenita's hair had been shaved on one side for the surgery, and they had fixed her hair in a way that covered that spot.

Everyone loved the coffin. It had a mirror on the side of it so that even those sitting down could see the body. In the end, the owners of the funeral home had been so moved that they gave me the casket at a little above their cost. Because the viewing and the funeral would not be held in the funeral home, but in the church, they would not be using their electricity or their janitorial service to clean up their viewing salon, so they gave us an additional discount.

Every night we had services in the church for those who came to pay their last respects to Nenita. Then the funeral service was conducted on July 15, the day before my birthday.

Later, my wife's cousin said to me, "You need to be in your office in the morning, because I'm going to deliver your wife's surprise birthday gift to you."

"Oh, what's that?" I asked.

"It's something she wanted you to have for your office," she said. "She ordered it and asked me not to tell you about it."

I went to my office that next morning in tears. Nenita's cousin had a furniture store, and she had gone there and ordered a nice set of mahogany furniture for the sitting area of the office. She wanted it to be nice so that when the parents of the school students came in, they would be blessed. There was a sofa, three chairs, and a coffee table, and they were all beautiful.

"I don't think I can have it here, reminding me of her," I said, but my children wouldn't hear of it.

"Mommy wanted you to have them," they insisted, so I relented.

"Let's celebrate your birthday," the children said.

But I said, "No, I don't feel like celebrating." At the moment, I wasn't sure if I could ever celebrate again.

52

I had been able to hold up fairly well at the church each evening, but when I would get home, I would lock myself in my room and cry uncontrollably.

The children were wonderful through all of this. Joy said to the younger ones, "Daddy is having a hard time. Let's try to be tough for his sake." They tried their very best to suppress their own pain when I was around and, instead, to comfort me.

Somehow I was not thinking of them at all. Surely they were going through their own terrible moments of grief, but I was unaware of it. I had some of Nenita's clothes piled on the bed, and I would lie down on top of them and sob.

Sometimes I pounded on the floor in my anguish. In those moments, the children called to me to ask if there was anything they could do, but I had locked the door so that no one could come in. I wanted no intrusion upon my personal grief. What could children know of the depths of a husband's loss? "No," I would answer. "I just want to be alone."

David seemed to be having a harder time with this than the girls. Sometimes he would scream out in the middle of the night. I would rush to his room to find that he was having a nightmare that his mother was visiting him, standing there by his feet, and putting the blanket over him. Still, I was not aware of how deeply my children were suffering until one day I received a call from the school.

One of Leah's teachers, a trained counselor, wanted to tell me that Leah was having some problems in school. I was surprised by this because Leah had always been extremely well behaved.

Fortunately, this counselor had taken time to speak with Leah, and Leah had poured out her heart about her loss. "You need to sit down with your children," the counselor told me, "and be honest with them about what you are feeling. You need to ask them to be honest with you and express what they are feeling. What you do now will affect them, for good or ill, the rest of their lives."

I took the wise counsel of this woman and sat down that night with the children to talk, but we didn't get very far. Joy began crying, and then we all began crying, and that's about as far as we got. When I told the counselor this the next day, she said that it was a good start.

"But I can't talk about it," I said. "I just cry."

"That's fine," she said. "Cry, but don't hold back your emotions around the children."

Another person was used to help me during those days. He was an American friend, Bill Van Breamer. He was the man who had lived in our house in San Francisco for many years, had helped us when we moved to Michigan and when we moved some things back to San Francisco. He arrived in Manila for the funeral, but after seeing the depths of my grief, he offered to come and live with us and take care of the house for a time.

Bill's presence was very important to the children during that time. They trusted him because he had often baby-sat with them while they were growing up in San Francisco, and he had come to Michigan to visit us several times a year. He was like a member of the family. One day he sat me down and scolded me. He told me that if I didn't snap out of my despair I would lose my children.

"Ray," he said to me, "for the sake of your children, you cannot continue like this. You have to get out and do something."

From then on, when the children went off to school and I would lock myself in the room, he would come and try to get me out of the house. "Let's go," he would say, "you need to get out of here."

Before long, Bill became convinced that we needed to move. "You have too many memories in this place," he said. I spoke with the children, and they agreed. They still didn't want to be far from the orphanage, but they did think it was a good idea for us to move to a different house.

"I'm not going home until we find you another place to live," Bill said.

I said, "But you could lose your job."

"I don't care," he said. "If I lose my job, I lose my job, but I'm not leaving until you find a suitable place."

But it took longer to find a suitable place than we both anticipated, and I eventually had to suggest that Bill go on home. "I'm fine now," I told him. I was preaching regularly again, and I would go to the church every day and work in my office at least half a day. Then I would go home, but at least I didn't just go into a corner to mourn. It was nearly August, and I was feeling much better. So, Bill went home, and the children and I kept looking for a place to move.

Before much more time had passed, we found a house in a nice subdivision called North Greenhills, and we moved. Bill was happy to hear it. He had something else important to say, "Ray, I've decided to come back and stay with you for a year to make sure you are doing well, or for however long I'm needed. I want to help you because you have too much responsibility right now for any one man."

"You can't do that," I said. "You're working."

"I'll quit my job," he countered.

"But I don't have money to pay you," I protested.

"It's okay. I'll be living with you and eating your food. I want to help you, and I want to help the children. You go ahead and get settled in your new place, and I'll be over within a couple of months."

True to his word, Bill quit his job and came to live and work with us. He proved to be an excellent supervisor for the orphanage, and I was able to turn that work over to him and know that it would be well managed. I would still be responsible for raising the funds for the home, but at least somebody would be there to supervise everything else.

Bill did much more than that. When he said to me one day, "I want to help you in the church," I was relieved. He helped us in many wonderful ways in the coming years.

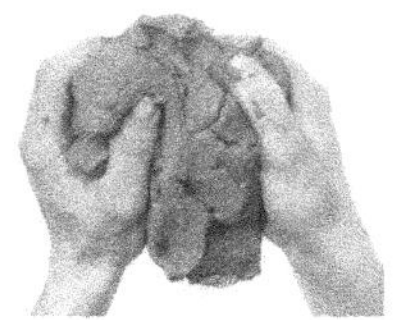

53

Before Nenita died, she had gotten to know Joy's boyfriend, Steve McKinney. He was the son of missionaries, and he and Joy had gotten to know each other in school. After graduation, Joy decided that she didn't want to go on to college at the moment. She and Steve wanted to get married.

I wasn't so sure about this. Although my sister thought that Joy was quite a young lady and that it was better for her to get married now, I was hesitant. Joy was only eighteen. My idea had been to send her to the States to live with my sister and go to college.

I agreed to meet the boy's parents, and I was very impressed. They were a fine missionary family.

It was interesting. Steve had been born in the United States, but when he was just eighteen months old, his parents had gone to the Philippines as missionaries. So, Steve had grown up in the Philippines. Joy, on the other hand, had been born in the Philippines, but when she was just eighteen months old, we had gone to Guam as missionaries. Then, she had grown up in the United States. Steve, an American, was more Filipino than Joy, and Joy, born in the Philippines, was more American then Steve.

I found Steve to be a fine Christian young man, but when I talked to him and Joy about my idea of her studying in the States, he very frankly told me, "We don't want to be apart from each other." And the marriage was set.

After the wedding, it was decided that Steve and Joy would move back to the States, and since his parents were going home on furlough, they could all live together. "If you would like to live in San Francisco," I told them, "I have a house there. Since Uncle Bill is living here with us, you could ask the other tenants to move, and you could have the whole house if you wanted it." They liked that idea.

"But, if we don't like San Francisco," Steve added, "we can always move to Seattle and rent an apartment together there." As it turned out, they didn't like San Francisco. It wasn't as Joy remembered it in her childhood, and they moved on to Seattle.

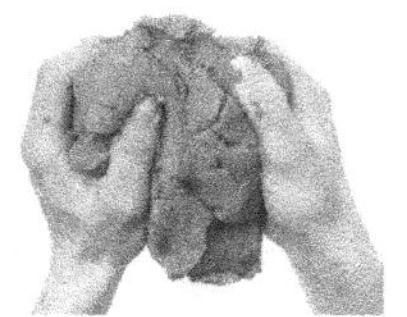

54

After Steve and Joy moved to the States, our landlord announced that he was raising our rent (very possibly because we had an American living with us). I thought the new rent was too much, so we again went in search of a place to live. In Pasig, we found a beautiful house belonging to the Filipino Ambassador to Vienna. Each of the three bedrooms upstairs was large, and each one had its own bathroom. The bedroom downstairs also had a bathroom, a very large one. Bill could live downstairs, and David and Leah and I could each have our own room upstairs. There was a family room, a dining room, a living room, a patio, and a garage. And this place was even a little bit cheaper than the rent we would have been paying in the other place. We took it.

The children loved living in Greenhills because some of their classmates lived nearby. If they missed the bus, they could ride with the other parents. But life went on, and we were blessed. The orphanage continued to grow, and the school continued to grow. We now had about a hundred and thirty-five students.

We had combined two classes under the ACE system, allowing one monitor to monitor two groups moving at different paces. The children worked on their own and only asked help as they needed it. I discovered, however, that this system was not very well suited to the Filipino culture, and I had been telling people that I felt we needed a major upgrade of the quality of our schooling.

We were using the sanctuary for classrooms. We had students who were coming from non-Christian homes, and many of them were being saved, and their parents were being saved as well. We also had students from non-Pentecostal churches, and they and their parents were being filled with the Holy Ghost. This was causing the church to grow even more.

Although the school, the orphanage and the church were all growing, the financial income had not kept pace with our growth. As I noted earlier, the church had been able to support itself for some time, and it was now doing much to support the school. Our tuition fees had always been low because we wanted it to be a missionary school, and we liked the idea of helping the poor. But because it was helping to support the school, the church had never been able to also fully support the orphanage.

Our principal resigned because of health problems, and I took over that position for a time. Only then did I realize how critical the financial situation was at the school. The bills were sometimes overwhelming, to the point that I thought if I didn't go to the United States and raise some support for the school, we would not be able to continue. I decided that I would make two trips a year.

Through all of this, our American friends had been generous. The churches in West Virginia had sent us towels and bedding for the orphanage, toys and even bicycles. Faith Tabernacle in Chicago had made many shipments to us, including a van that we used for the church and the school. Pastor Michael Enerson of Full Gospel Temple in Westland, Michigan rented twenty-foot container, filled it with all sorts of supplies, and sent it over. But the needs kept increasing. Now I made some contacts in the U.S. and said that I would be coming.

Jack Kincaid had me at the television station in Clarksburg, and he raised more than $25,000. While I was there, other pastors heard me and invited me to their churches. I was able to preach, for instance, at First Assembly of God Church in Fairmont. The pastor was away on a mission trip to South America, and I was asked if I would preach on a Sunday night. That afternoon, we had a telethon at the station, and that night I preached in Fairmont, and they gave me a very good offering.

As always, the Millers gave me a generous offering, and the other churches were very liberal as well. Aside from the money, people were giving many things for the orphanage, especially many wonderful books for the library. It was a very fruitful trip, to say the least.

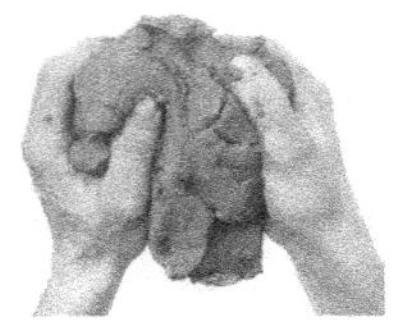

55

As people got saved in the church, many of them went back to their provinces when they had opportunity and preached there. Some of those who were fruits of that outreach came to the capital to our services to be baptized. We were continually raising up workers in the church, and after we filled our immediate leadership needs, we began to send these new people out to other places to minister. Little by little, this had developed into a serious church-planting program. Before it was over, we had planted some thirty churches, and another fifteen or more had allied themselves with us.

I was also going out to minister in other places myself around the country and around the world. Particularly, I had begun making trips to Viet Nam, China, and India. This had all been extremely helpful to me in my recovery. I was busy because God was opening more doors to us.

About this time, we began finding our facilities in Manila very cramped. We looked for a new principal, and we found Mrs. Estella Maranen, who had been the vice-principal of another school. I said to her, "We need you, and you meet our qualifications, but we cannot afford to pay you what you are worth. If you will agree to come with us for what we can pay you now, when the school progresses and prospers, I promise that you will prosper with it." For now, her salary would be coming from the church, not the school. Thank God that she agreed to my offer.

Even at the rate our teachers were paid, the payroll for the school had always been a problem. When Fridays came, I had to run here and there getting money together to cover it. I was often using fully half of our family support for the needs of this ministry. Some people sent us generous special love offerings of five hundred and a thousand dollars, but the needs never stopped rising. Although God never left us in any moment, sometimes the financial strains caused us to feel that there was no hope of ever getting ahead. And sometimes the Lord allowed us to go through some very trying periods.

Another thing that forced our hand and caused us to start believing for a larger building was that the Department of Education told us that we could not continue the school because it was in a commercial area. A shopping mall was not a suitable site for a school, they said. We needed to build a larger building, and we began accumulating funds for that purpose.

Our new principal said to me one day, "Pastor Ray, I understand why you have wanted to keep the tuitions low to help the poor, but not all of the students who are coming are from poor families. The school began for the orphans, but now it is far more than the orphans. I feel that we need to increase the tuition."

Raise the tuition? That was a novel idea to me.

She explained, "How can you hire good quality teachers if you don't have money to work with? To bring up the standard of the school, you must hire some good quality teachers. We can still serve the orphans and the poor for free, but let's charge the same as other schools to our other students."

"Upgrading the curriculum is my great concern," I told her.

"I know it, and I can do that," she answered, "if we have more money to work with. I promise you that if you will care for the spiritual life of the school, I will see to it that there is a curriculum that you can be proud of." I sensed that she could do it, for she was a very gifted person.

"That's fine with me," I said. "Let's give it a try."

Mrs. Maranen soon went to the Department of Education and asked how much we could raise our tuitions. They told her that we could have a fifteen percent raise, so we raised our tuitions by fifteen percent before enrollment time that year, and that proved to be the thing that broke the financial barrier for us. For the first time, the school was able to stand on its own two feet, and this allowed me to concentrate my fund-raising efforts more on the orphanage.

The curriculum of the school was wonderfully upgraded, to a powerful program we could all be proud of. Chapel services were just as powerful as ever, and memory verses were worked into every lesson. The teachers were required to teach their students songs of worship and to help them learn portions of God's Word.

We still applied some of the standards that we had learned from the ACE program, but our program was now much more suited to the people we were serving. We had taken some very important steps for the future.

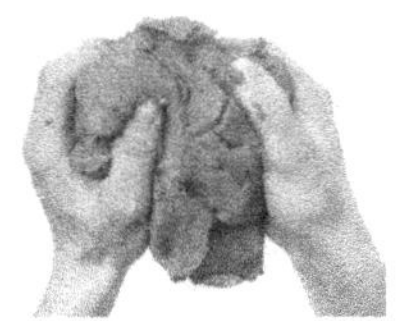

56

As enrollment continued to increase in the school, it put more pressure on us to find a larger place. Just about then, a wealthy man was saved and started attending our church. Because he was still young in the Lord, he asked me to visit him in his home and disciple him. I was extremely busy and wasn't able to do as much as I would have liked, but I did go to the man's house once in a while to share with him. One day he handed me a check and said, "This is for your ministry." It was a little less than a million pesos (during that time, the value of the peso was seventeen or eighteen to a dollar), so that was a lot of money.

"This," I said, "is the beginning of our building fund," and I was determined not to touch it for any other purpose. Before long, the man handed me another check, this one for eight hundred thousand pesos, adding substantially to our bank account.

We were encouraged to look for a suitable property, and we found one with nine hundred and sixty-six square meters, more than ten thousand square feet. The site was perfect, and the location was wonderful for both a church and a school. It had only one problem. The price tag, as with all properties in that vast metropolis, was sky high. The total cost would be six million, eight hundred thousand pesos. And we had accumulated less than two million.

"But," I told our people, "the building we put up there will not only be our school; it will be for the church as well. This is worthy of our investment."

We announced to the parents that we would be purchasing land for a new school, and some of those who were able gave toward it. Others agreed to take part in a fund-raising project. The principal sat down with them, and they discussed how this could be accomplished. First, a brochure would be drawn up. It was felt that I could use the same brochure in my fund-raising trips to the States.

On that brochure, we wanted a likeness of the actual building we would be putting up, so plans began to be formulated for a four-story building. This proposed building, unlike many facilities in our country, would not skimp to save money. It would be beautiful, and it would honor the Lord.

Some of the parents began to raise funds among their friends, and they had some success. Other money came in practically unsolicited. Steve Murell, a missionary who was pastoring in the Philippines, called and told me, "Pastor, we're excited about what you're doing, and we want to give you fifty thousand pesos to help." This was the smoothest fund-raising I had ever seen. But, by the time we were ready to settle for the land, we still didn't have enough cash raised. We had to tell the owners of the land that we knew God was going to do a miracle for us.

The land belonged to a corporation formed of the brothers and sisters of a large family. Their business ventures had failed, so they needed to sell the land and split the proceeds. One of the sisters was a member of our church, and I asked her if she and her brothers and sisters might be able to hold the mortgage on the land. We would give them the down payment we had saved up, and instead of going to the bank for the rest, we would pay the owners monthly payments. She said it would be fine with her, but she didn't think her siblings would agree to it. Some of them were leaving the country and needed their money in cash.

"Please talk to them," I suggested, "and see what we can work out." She asked, but the others were not able to do us this favor.

One day one of the school parents, a businessman, was having lunch with some business associates at a restaurant in the famous Manila Hotel. In the course of the conversation, this man brought out the brochure we had prepared for the fund-raiser and told his friends about what we were doing to enlarge the outreach of the church and school. "Can I make a donation?" one of his friends asked.

"Sure you can," the man answered. "And God will bless you for it. We believe in the principle of giving so that the Lord can prosper and bless us. If you give, there is no way that we can repay you, but the Lord will repay you many times over."

The friend was excited by this prospect. "Well, how much do you think I should donate?" he asked.

"Whatever the Lord lays upon your heart," the businessman said.

The man pulled out his checkbook and wrote a check for a hundred thousand pesos.

That night, the businessman got home very late. In fact, it was already midnight (very late in our country), but he called me anyway. "I'm sorry to call so late," he told me, "but I need to tell you something. I have a check in my hand for the building project for a hundred thousand pesos. The man who wrote it is not even a Christian, but the Lord touched his heart, and he wanted to do it." We rejoiced together.

"Do you want me to bring the check over now?" he asked. "Or shall I just drop it by the school office tomorrow morning when I drop my children off for their classes?"

"Tomorrow will be fine," I told him. "I'll be there early, for the flag ceremony and the chapel service."

Several days later, the two men met again, and the friend told the businessman that since he had given the hundred-thousand-peso donation, many good things had opened up to him. "I have already received more than I gave. Can I give more?" And he gave another hundred thousand pesos.

The parents had a concert to raise money, and other methods were used as well. Still, we eventually were forced to apply for a loan. A lady in the church told me that she could put up her property as a guarantee to borrow a hundred and ninety-thousand pesos of the amount needed. She was willing to do that if the church would make the monthly payments.

Other people were donating good quality jewelry for us to sell for the building project. The excitement was building, both among those within the church and others who were not yet members. Even the children in the school were praying to make it all happen.

I knew the loan officer of one particular bank to be a believer, and I approached her and told her our situation. "We're not accustomed to loaning money to churches," she told me. "What would we do if there was a failure of payment? How could we collect? It's too risky. But, let us look at it and see if there is anything we can do for you."

The amount we needed to finance was nearly four million pesos, an unheard of thing in our country for a church, but we were praying that God would move on the hearts of the bank officials to give us a miracle. To help us qualify for such a large loan, we submitted the combined income of the church, the school, and the orphanage.

"Having the orphanage in there might touch the heart of these people," the loan officer told us. "When they know how you are helping the poor, maybe they will be moved."

We waited a long time while the bank board considered our request. In fact, it seemed like forever. They asked for this document and that until it seemed that we had submitted every conceivable document. In the process, however, I felt that I was getting worn down.

Some of our people were golfers, and they were going to Baguio to play for a few days. "Come and go along with us," they suggested. I wasn't a golfer, but I agreed to go because I needed a break.

The other men took their wives along, and we all stayed together in one house. "Pastor, relax," they said, and they proceeded to try to make me comfortable.

One of the men who went with us was talking one day about the land we wanted to buy. "I have some land myself," he said. "It's part of an inheritance and will be divided between many members of our family, but we haven't been able to sell it. Pray that I will be able to sell that land, and I will give a hundred thousand pesos for the church building project." When we got back to town, I alerted our prayer warriors to lift up this need before the Lord. One more gift like that could put us over the top.

God did the miracle for us. The man sold his land, and he kept his promise to God. This enabled us to finally move forward and finalize our purchase of the property in San Juan. With that, the bank approved our loan. Within a year the property would be totally paid off.

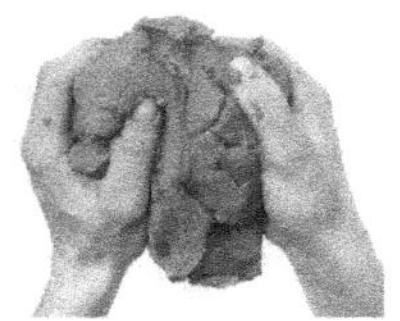

57

One Sunday morning we all marched with a police escort from the old church location to the new property for the ground-breaking ceremony. It was a long procession that created a great traffic jam. We sang and worshiped the Lord as we did that victory march. Not long after the ground-breaking, I left for the United States to raise funds for the new building.

The church in San Francisco gave us $25,000 for the building, and other churches added their amount, so that I was able to raise about $100,000 in a few weeks time. With the exchange rate now at forty-five pesos to the dollar, it was a substantial beginning.

Local people also began to give. Even the owner of the construction company we hired to build the church donated five hundred thousand pesos. The brother of one of the men who gave the largest amounts for the building had a cement factory, and consequently all of the cement in the construction (valued at nearly two million pesos) was given free. The miracles just kept coming. What miracles God was doing!

Still, on three different occasions during the months ahead, the money ran out, and I felt I had to tell the architect in the morning that this would be the last day of work. We would have to stop the construction temporarily until more funds came in. "We'll let you know when we can resume the work," I told him. Then I would call our people to prayer.

On the first occasion I did this, before the day was over, a miracle had happened, another hundred-thousand peso offering had been given, and we were able to continue the work.

On the second occasion, when I spoke with the workers about discontinuing the work, it was because we had no more money for materials. They were running out that day. I went to one of our suppliers of steel reinforcing bars and sand and gravel and asked if he could give us credit. He agreed to give us thirty days to pay, and the work was able to continue.

By the third time I told the workers that the work would have to stop, they no longer believed me. They thought I was just "talking tough." They were sure the construction would go on, and it did. To provide the money, God was using people we didn't even know. Some of them were unbelievers.

The parents were continuing their fund-raising program for the school. At one point, we needed two hundred and fifty thousand to continue, and another church gave it. The children of the pastor of that church were attending our school, and they liked it a lot. We continued to rejoice. Within fifteen months, the building had advanced sufficiently that we felt we could begin to use the lower floor for our services as we continued to work on the rest of the building. Such a use was not forbidden there as it is here in the United States. There were no windows in the building yet, but we didn't want to continue paying rent in the previous location. That thirty-five thousand pesos a month could help us finish the building. For the time being, the school would stay where it was.

We again marched from the old location to the new as we began our first Sunday morning service in the new locale, and again it was a glorious march of victory.

Finishing such a large and expensive building was a constant challenge. On one occasion, we fell nearly sixty days behind with our supplier, and he said, "We cannot deliver any more materials until you pay this sixty-day account." The overdue amount was nearly two hundred thousand pesos. I was praying for a miracle.

The architect who had designed the building was a member of the church, and he was also a businessman. One day, he said to me, "Pastor Ray, I can borrow money that will cover that, but we would need to return it within three or four weeks."

I said, "Good, do it!"

"They might charge us a little interest," he said.

"That's okay," I said. "Do it." We paid the supplier, and he delivered more materials, but then we had to decide how we were going to pay back the two-hundred-thousand peso loan.

For years, we had been doing a lot with evangelistic outreaches, and I told the congregation that we could not stop now just because we were in the midst of a construction project. We still needed to continue the ministry God had entrusted to us.

The school was gaining more students, but now we were able to pay the teachers on time, and the church was not strained any more to subsidize the school. Things were going better, but now we had to make a push to finish the building. We were now working on the roof of the second floor.

58

Sometimes we had very unusual trials, and with them, very unusual miracles. For instance, I was busy at the construction site one day when I was told there was an important phone call from Bill at the orphanage. When I got to the phone, Bill said, "Pastor Ray, we have a big problem over here. It's already 11:30, and we have nothing to feed the children for lunch."

"Why are you just now telling me this?" I asked. "Never mind. I'm on my way."

I was sure there must be some rice in the house and something else that could go with it, so I went there quickly to look around. Bill was right. The refrigerator was empty, the freezer was empty, and there wasn't so much as a grain of rice in the place. I scolded Bill, "You should have told me. The children cannot be expected to delay their lunch. What do we do now?"

On top of all that, they had run out of formula for the babies. When the kids had seen me, they called out, "Daddy Pastor, Daddy Pastor." They wanted to play with me like usual, but I told them we had something serious to do right then.

I had some of the workers take the children outside and keep them busy so that they would not think about being hungry. There was one box of biscuits that could be shared among them as they played. But what to do for the babies?

"Boil some water and put a little honey in it," I told those who cared for the little ones. "Maybe that will quiet them for a while, until we can come up with a better solution."

Suddenly, I had a terrible headache. I was perplexed. "Lord, what will we do?"

I had seen some bones in the freezer, so I told someone to start making soup with those bones. "Put some salt and pepper in it," I said. "At least it will taste good. I will go find something more substantial for the evening meal. It's so late that there is nothing more we can do."

As one o'clock neared, the children began coming in saying that they were hungry. They were told that "the soup" was almost ready. Then, when "the soup" was ready, we called for the children to all come in and take their seats. That day we had sixty-two children, plus staff, to feed.

When everyone was seated, I looked at my watch: one-fifteen. Everyone was looking at me, so I said, "Let's pray," and I started to bow my head, but then I stopped and turned back to the children. "Daddy Pastor has nothing to put on your plate today, but I know that Daddy God will give us our food. We must trust Him."

I'm not sure that little children understood the theological implications of all that, but then we prayed. I purposely prolonged my prayer a little that day, for I was not anxious for the children to taste their bone "soup."

Most of the children were very reverent as I prayed, but a few of them lost patience and began banging their plates. Clearly, they were hungry. Apparently, the moment of truth was about to arrive.

Before I could finish praying, the doorbell rang, and one of the workers went out to answer it. Another lady, the main cook, followed. Then, from the entrance way, I heard both of them screaming.

I quickly ended my prayer, and asked, "What's wrong with them?"

It sounded more like shouting than screaming, and the lady who did the cooking ran in to say, "Pastor, come. There's a Chinese man here. His truck is loaded with food, and he wants to see you."

I went to the door and met the man. He was very apologetic at first. "We were a bit delayed in coming," he said, and then he showed me what he and his people had brought. There was fried chicken, pork, and vegetables, fried rice and noodles. It was all cooked and ready to eat. And there were fruits and juices.

There was also an abundance of uncooked food: three huge sacks of rice, one of sugar, vegetables, fruits and canned goods. There were treats of every type, and there was powdered milk for the babies.

"Where shall we put it all?" He asked. I told them to put the cooked foods on the table, and everyone began to eat.

When we had time to talk, I said to him, "You weren't late in coming. You were right on time."

"No," he insisted, "let me explain what I mean." He and his wife, who were from another church, owned a grocery store. Someone had told them about the work we were doing in the orphanage, and two weeks before they had felt that they needed to come and visit us and bring an offering of food. They were busy, and so they kept postponing their visit. That very morning, his wife had said to him, "If we keep postponing this, we will never do it. We need to do it today."

After thinking it over, she decided, "Instead of just taking them foods to prepare, I think we should cook everything and have it ready to eat."

"You were sent by God at just the right moment because we had nothing to give the children to eat today," I told him.

"Well, there is more where this came from," he said. "We'll come again in a few days and bring some more groceries. But if you need something before that time, please give us a call." Several days later they brought three more large sacks of rice, and we had enough of that important staple of the Filipino diet to last us for several months.

When the Chinese man left that day, we were all laughing and crying at once. I said, "Oh, God, You never fail."

Some of the smaller children were not able to understand what was happening that day, but the larger ones knew. "See how God provides for us," I told them. "You just need to continue praying and believing for His daily provision. He will never fail you." Suddenly I realized that my headache was gone, and I was feeling fine.

I didn't have to worry about the evening meal. There was more than enough. "I'm coming here to feast with you tonight," I told everyone, and I went back to the construction.

That evening, before I left for the orphanage, I received a phone call. "There are some foreigners here who would like to adopt Filipino babies," I was told. "Could they stop by the orphanage and talk to you?"

I said, "Sure," and gave them directions to get there.

The visitors came that night, and they brought cans of cookies and crackers with them. "We would like to see some of your children," they said.

"I appreciate your visit," I told them, "but we're not quite ready for adoption for our orphans yet. We still have some paperwork that needs to be filed with the government. Our social workers are concentrating on that now. Maybe we could recommend some other homes to you."

"That's kind of you," they answered, "but if you don't mind, we would still like to visit your orphanage." Before they left that night, they handed us several hundred dollars for the work.

"Let's get this changed into pesos and start a special orphanage account," I told my secretary. "We'll need this." It seemed that just when we were running out of money, the Lord always sent an angel our way to help us.

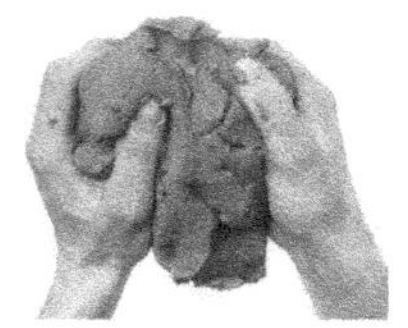

59

It took us eighteen months to finish the building, and it was truly amazing how we were able to generate the funds to do it. Word had gone out that the building was too large and too nice and that it would never be finished. "One day Ray will pack his bags and leave," some ministers had predicted, "and that will be the end of that building program." But God had been faithful. Now the church moved onto the upper level, and the school occupied the lower floor.

Once we had moved the school, the enrollment again shot up. Suddenly, we had three hundred and fifty paying students, representing many churches, and no one was complaining about the higher tuitions. The school was now self-sufficient and began helping to support the church, rather than the other way around.

We hadn't done all this without borrowing more money from the bank — ten million pesos in all. The building alone had ended up costing us US $1.8 million, and since the exchange rate was fifty pesos to one dollar, that meant the building had cost ninety million pesos. We had no problem financing ten million pesos of that.

Now, we just needed to make our monthly payments. For the first year, we were only able to pay the interest. That alone was nearly P183,000.00 a month. Within a few years time, however, largely due to the activities of the school, we were able to pay off the mortgage and have the property debt free. What a great miracle!

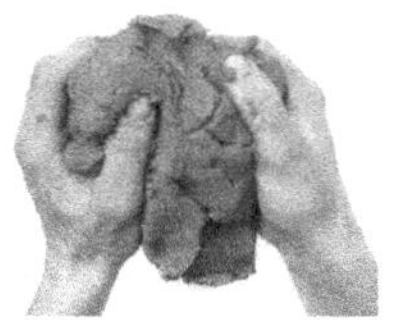

60

In the early months of 1996, I was invited to speak at a large missions conference conducted in one of the largest Assemblies of God churches in Fort Wayne, Indiana. Leah went with me, and on the way, we stopped in Chicago and went to visit Faith Tabernacle. Some of the leaders there said to me, "We need a pastor. Would you consider being our new pastor?"

"No way," I said. "I haven't had time to enjoy our new building in Manila." At the time, it was not yet totally finished. Although it was livable and everyone loved it, there was still some finishing work to be done, both inside and outside. We hadn't even been able to completely waterproof the roofs (because the cost was somewhere around half a million pesos.) "No, I'm afraid I could not do that," I told them. "I have my hands full in Manila."

They had me preach in the church that Saturday night, and they asked me to reconsider. I looked around. Faith Tabernacle was indeed a great church. It had a wonderful facility in downtown Chicago, a diverse congregation made up of people of many different nationalities, and a long history of faithful service to the community. But no, I could not consider their offer. Why should I? I was at a high point in our ministry in the Philippines, we had sacrificed much to get to this point, and it seemed all downhill from there.

The church was growing, the school was growing, and the orphanage was doing very well. Now that we were into our new facility, the pressure on me had lifted considerably. Now, I just wanted to enjoy the fruit of our labors for years to come.

But the leaders of Faith Tabernacle did not easily accept my answers. Some of them followed us to other meetings, and they spoke again with me there, and one of them, Kim Hill, called me — wherever I happened to be — Indiana, Michigan, and again after I had gotten back to Chicago. He kept trying to convince me that I should be the new pastor of Faith Tabernacle, and I kept insisting that, for many reasons, I simply could not do that.

Leah and I left Chicago and were on our way to San Francisco. From there, we would take a flight back to the Philippines. In the airplane, Leah said to me, "Dad, you'd better pray about this. This is both a big opportunity and a big temptation for you. I feel sorry for you, and I'd hate to be in your shoes."

But my consideration was not just for myself. The ministry the Lord had led us to start in the Philippines was large and still growing. Why should I think of leaving it? The truth, however, was that I had had an experience that I hadn't yet told anyone about, and it was haunting me now as Leah made her point.

Just before leaving for San Francisco we had been staying in the house of some friends in Skokie, Illinois. They had joined a ten-day tour to Israel, and, because they had no children, Leah and I had been left alone in their house. They had welcomed us to stay as long as we wanted and instructed us to just lock up and leave the key on a table when we decided to leave.

One night, while we were in that house, Leah had wanted to visit some friends, and the parents had invited her to spend the night, so she had told me she would be back the next day. This was fine with me. I was busy packing books that had been given for the school library and getting them ready for shipment to the Philippines. Eventually, I got tired and decided to lie down for a while on the couch and rest. I turned on the television and began to listen to a Morris Cerullo program, but my eyes soon closed, and I fell asleep.

I was awakened by the noise of the door clicking open. Leah had the key, so I called out, "Leah, is that you?"

No one answered.

I hadn't wanted to open by eyes, so I was about to drift off to sleep again when I heard the door click again. This time I rose up to see who was there, but mysteriously the door was still closed. *Well,* I thought, *it must have been the neighboring door.* Our friends lived in a condominium, and the two entrances were side by side in the hallway.

Then I heard footsteps, and my hair suddenly stood on end. I was numb and unable to move. I wanted to say something, but I couldn't. I tried to lift up my head and found that it was impossible. What was going on? This was not normal in any way. I closed my eyes again, trying to make sense of what was happening to me.

Then, somehow, I suddenly knew that it was the Lord I had heard come in, and I opened my eyes. I'm not sure what I expected to see in that moment, but I saw the Lord.

His presence was not distinct. It was more like a shadow, and I was not able to see a head or a face. All that I could see was His shape, outlined by His white robe. But I did see His hand extending from His side.

Then I heard His voice. He was saying, "Will you do it for Me?"

I was not able to respond.

Then, just as suddenly as He had come, He disappeared.

I burst into tears. I knew exactly what the Lord was talking about. He was asking me to move back to America and to take the pastorate at Faith Tabernacle, but I had no desire to come back.

Still, did I have a right to say no to the Lord? Didn't He know that I was always ready to do what He wanted me to do?

After that happened, I had made up my mind to go back to the Philippines, and if the Lord wanted to speak to me further, He could. "If these people follow me there or call me there," I told the Lord, "then I will know that this is Your will."

When we arrived in San Francisco, Kim Hill called me again. This time he asked if I would be willing to fly back and meet with the board and hear them out. "All we're asking is that you meet with us and that we pray about it together," he said. "Nothing more."

"But why go to all that expense," I asked him, "when you have no guarantee?"

"Just come and pray," he urged.

I was torn. Our flight was due to leave for the Philippines in five days and there were some things I wanted to do in San Francisco. Should I go back?

I went to preach for David Shebley in Stockton, California, and he confirmed to me what I was feeling. The call to Chicago was indeed of God. So, in the end, I flew back to Chicago and met with the board of Faith Tabernacle. They spoke of their vision for the future of the church and why they felt they wanted me to be their pastor. I said very little. "We'll pray about it," I promised, and I left the following morning. Four more days, and I will be home free, I thought.

The day before we were to leave for the Philippines, Kim called again. "Pastor," he said, "we really need you here. This is a large and thriving church, and we don't want to leave it to the wolves."

This time I felt constrained to respond. "Okay," I said, "I'll tell you. God has been speaking to me," and "I will come. I had intended to go back to Manila first, but let me see Leah off tomorrow, and I'll be there."

I didn't want to alarm our people in Manila, so I asked Leah not to say anything about what was developing at Faith Tabernacle in Chicago. She was only to say that I was taking a little time off and would be coming soon. It was now the third week of March, and I suggested that I might be home by Easter. Leah left for Manila on Thursday, and the next day, I again boarded a flight for Chicago.

When someone questioned Leah about my absence, she said what I had told her, but they concluded, "He's not coming back."

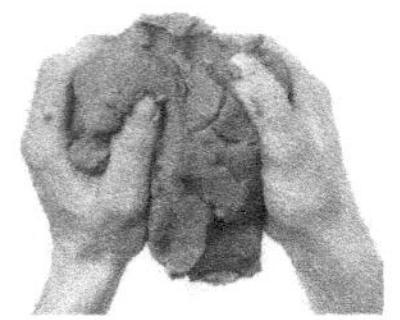

61

Our first Sunday service together in Chicago was Palm Sunday, and we powerfully celebrated together the triumphal entry of Christ. I felt like the timing could not have been better. I was introduced to the congregation of Faith Tabernacle as their new pastor, and I expressed my heart's desire to them about what I envisioned God doing through the church and through them.

Faith Tabernacle was a very exciting church with great potential. I had never pastored a truly international church before, but this was one. Perhaps ninety percent of the congregation was made up of African-Americans and blacks of Jamaica, the Caribbean, and Africa, but there were more than forty-five nationalities represented. We were Japanese, Chinese, Filipino, Hispanics, Polish, German, and Romanians. We had to conduct many services. On any one Sunday, our attendance in the several services was running two thousand to two thousand five hundred in four services.

The church had its beginnings some forty years before with the Charismatic Renewal and a member of the Full Gospel Business Men's Fellowship by the name of Henry Carlson. Brother Carlson was an ad executive, but he allowed God to use him. First, he began meeting with a few other people in a house, but this grew until he eventually purchased a large and popular boxing arena in downtown Chicago and converted it into a church.

Morris Cerullo was the first evangelist to preach there, and he helped the small congregation raise money for their payment on the property. After Henry, who pastored the church for twenty years, there were several other pastors, then Al Smith, then myself. I was only the fifth pastor in the more than forty year history of the church.

Many good words of prophecy had been spoken over Faith Tabernacle, that it would make an impact around the world. I was excited, and my enthusiasm was contagious. I sensed a great excitement in the congregation that day. Surely others would join our vision, and we would accomplish great things for God.

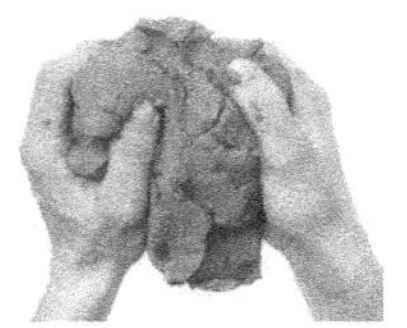

62

THE NEXT HURDLE WAS HOW TO ADVISE OUR PEOPLE IN MANILA, AT the church, the school, and the orphanage, that I had decided to make such a drastic move. After that glorious Easter Service at Faith Tabernacle, I flew to San Francisco and from there proceeded on back to the Philippines.

Soon after I arrived, I got alone with my senior assistant, Pastor Sunday Taniega, and told him that there was now to be a changing of the guard, a passing of the baton. "It's time for me to go." I told him.

Pastor Sunday was in tears. He had been saved in the church, and little by little I had groomed him for the ministry. He had now been working with me for twelve years already. It was a very powerful moment.

Next, I called all the pastoral staff and told them that Pastor Sunday would be taking over the leadership. I asked them not to spread the word yet.

Next, I gathered the board members and let them know of my decision. They were fully behind me. Then I called the workers, the volunteers, and I shared this change with them. We were all crying, and it was a sad moment, but I told them, "You know that this ministry is not just mine; this is the Lord's ministry. In the natural, I don't want to leave because I have laid down my life here, and I have invested much into this work." (When Nenita died, I had taken some $45,000 from the insurance money I received and put it into the building. I had also withdrawn money from our children's college funds to invest there.)

"But," I continued, "I cannot disobey the Lord's orders." I asked them not to spread the word around, to let me tell the people that Sunday.

"How long will you be away this time, Pastor?" one of my board members asked me with tears.

"I'm not talking about a trip," I told them all. "This is indefinite. I am resigning as your pastor and passing the torch to Pastor Sunday."

"Surely you will not completely abandon us," they protested. "Pastor Sunday is a good man, but he's still very young. We need your help. Will you not agree to supervise us?"

"I am not disappearing from the earth," I told them. "Pastor Sunday can always write me or call me whenever he needs to. I will not be completely cut off from my relationship with you. But, on the other hand, I can no longer be your pastor, and Pastor Sunday will now be the one you will look to."

We combined the two services on Sunday morning so that I could speak to everyone at once. It was a very sad moment, and we were all crying. "This man is now your pastor," I said to them, bringing Pastor Sunday forward. "I believe my job here is over, and it is time for me to move on. This, then, represents the moment of the changing of the guard, the passing of the baton."

Fearing the worst, the workers had brought towels to wipe their tears. Their eyes were all red from weeping. Some of them, I had been told, had been crying all night long.

"Now," I said to them all, "I need you to release me, and I need for you to pray for me from this day forward. I will still be here for two more weeks, but not as your pastor." The minutes of our board meeting had stated that Pastor Sunday would take over effective that Sunday, and that's the way we did it.

It was a strange two weeks. This was my home, and yet it was not my home. God had called me to a new field of endeavor, and I trusted His decision.

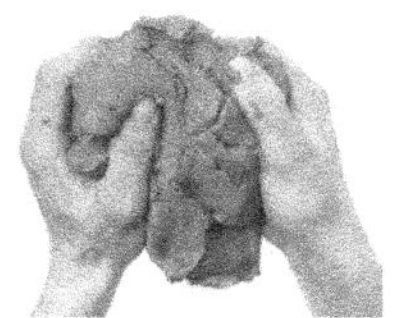

63

TWO WEEKS LATER I FLEW BACK TO CHICAGO AND BEGAN THE WORK IN earnest. In every service, I encouraged the people to open their hearts to God and believe to be used more than ever before. Gradually, the spirit rose in our midst until every service was a wonderful adventure, one in which many people were saved, healed and delivered.

But as excited as I was about being the pastor of such a great church, I was quickly made aware of the serious problems the church faced. It looked like the church was in imminent danger of splitting into many pieces. Some of the members had become demoralized over the finances and were seriously threatening to leave. I was sure that we could overcome these difficulties and bring the congregation back into fruitfulness, but it would be a challenge.

Concerning the finances, the day before that Palm Sunday service, I had learned that the church was deeply in debt. There was a mortgage of $1.8 million, and the payment on it had not been made in six months. There was also a loan of $150,000, with a large balloon payment due in August. The bank had wanted to foreclose on the church, but they didn't know how to go about it since, in their mind, the church was a community property, and they didn't want to upset the community.

There were three properties involved with the mortgage: the church, the parsonage, and a house the church owned at the back of the property and rented to members. They were all at risk and needed to be set free from the bank lien.

That Palm Sunday service was beautiful, and I preached from Joel 2:21-28. That passage said we had nothing to fear. God was about to do new and marvelous things. It also spoke of days of suffering and scarcity, want and lack, but it said those days were coming to an end. Why? Because God had promised abundance. He would restore all that the devil had taken away.

Based on God's promises, I assured the members that the reproach the church had suffered in the community would be lifted, and we would no longer be a laughing stock in that great city. Indeed, we would be favored by the Lord and would be a blessing to the city of Chicago and beyond.

Even though the attendance at the church had fallen off dramatically, along with the giving, I encouraged the people to honor the Lord with their gifts by giving their very best. I let them know that we were giving to God and not to man and that He would reward them. That day marked a turnaround in the fortunes of the church. The offering that day was phenomenal in the first service, this continued in the second service, and even increased in the third service. (The Sunday evening services had been canceled because of low attendance, but we would soon bring them back.) On that first Sunday, in the three services, we raised between $80,000 and $90,000.

As the accountant and treasurer and their assistants were counting the money from the first service, they were jumping and shouting for joy. When I went up to my office, which was next to the finance office, I knocked on the door to find out what the commotion was all about. I found them all weeping and rejoicing. It had been many months since they had seen that kind of response from the congregation. When they told me that the offering from the first service had been more than $30,000, the Lord said to me, "What I promise that I will do." His plan of rescue for Faith Tabernacle was unfolding before my eyes.

I had announced in that Palm Sunday service that Easter Sunday would be our breakthrough Sunday, a Sunday of new beginnings for us, and the beginning of God's deliverance for the church and for the people. I encouraged everyone to bring their special Resurrection Sunday tithes and offerings, and I told them to invite people who had left the church to come back.

That next Sunday, the second Sunday I was there, Easter Sunday, the church was nearly filled in every service. I chose that day to tell the people about the $1.8 million mortgage and the $150,000 loan plus interest and the balloon payment that had to be made in August. Some of the people were understandably upset that they had not known about this indebtedness. One man called out, "What happened to the money we gave toward the payment of the mortgage? We thought the mortgage was paid."

I could only answer, "I wasn't here during that time, so I can't answer that, but I do know this is what we owe. As the new pastor, it's now my responsibility to pay this off and set the church free from the control of the bank. If you love this church, you need to help pay off the mortgage. Your house is connected to this house, and if you bless the House of the Lord, your house will also be blessed."

I asked for pledges that day, telling the people I believed we could pay off the total indebtedness in three years. The pledges we raised that day amounted to nearly $500,000, and some of it came in cash.

We recorded the names, addresses, and phone numbers of the people who pledged so that the office staff could follow up with them. In the other services, many also pledged their help. In each service in the coming months, we received the pledge money separate from the other offerings, and I announced each week the progress we had made on paying down the debt.

We had a radio program, and on that program, we asked the people to pray for us and, if they were able, to help us pay down the debt. Some donations came in, even from other churches. People who were listening to the program started attending Faith Tabernacle and giving in the offerings.

I was invited to preach in many other churches, big and small, in the city. Many times I was interviewed on Channel 38, the Christian TV station there in Chicago. At times I was called on to do the devotions for all the workers in the station. This all brought more attention to the church, more people coming, and better offerings.

We began having campmeetings every summer and brought in special speakers. Keith Butler, from one of the largest churches in the Detroit area, came, the well-known author, John Bevere, came and spoke for us, and Paula White's husband came and spoke in our conference. The church was in revival, and we were thriving.

We had the $150,000 loan paid off before August, and in three year's time we were able to have a special service to burn the mortgage.

Because of their generous giving, many of the Faith Tabernacle people were able to buy homes and others paid off their mortgages. I had challenged them, "If you want your house to be free from the bank, you need to release the House of God from the bank first." And it happened.

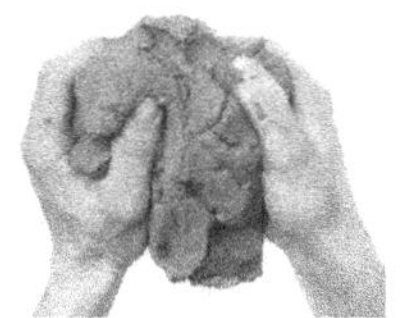

64

When we were close to paying off the mortgage, the president of the bank called me one day. He said, "How did you do this? Not only have you nearly paid off the mortgage, but this is the first time the church has deposited so much in the bank."

I said, "Well, I didn't do it. It's the Lord who did it."

He offered me a new line of credit that day and said we could borrow up to $1 million. I declined. "We won't be borrowing again," I told him. "Once we pay off the balance we owe, we don't want to be bound by debt anymore."

From the moment we paid off the mortgage, Faith Tabernacle operated as a debt-free church. Very quickly I challenged the people to do a complete remodeling. "We keep fixing the heating and cooling systems, but they're too old and need to be replaced," I told them. "This sanctuary needs to be remodeled. I want to change the light fixtures, and all the chairs need to be replaced. (They were bright orange, and we needed a neutral color.) The fellowship hall has to be fixed and some of the classrooms." We started getting pledges for the remodeling of the building, inside and outside. Outside there were some cracks and some leaks to be repaired. Within seven months we had remodeled everything, and we had paid as we went. Even though the total cost was about $600,000, we didn't have to borrow a dime.

The church was being blessed and also having an impact on the community at large. Before we began the restoration, some of the other pastors in the city were wondering if the church might be padlocked, but the Lord did not allow that to happen.

Now, after we had paid off the mortgage and did the remodeling, we were able to launch new ministries. We started a feeding program for the homeless and medical treatment for the poor of the community (utilizing the doctors in the congregation). Utilizing the lawyers in the congregation, we opened a legal service for those who could not afford a lawyer. This was broadcast throughout the community and brought in more people, who then got saved. We also opened a pantry that provided groceries for people in need. At Thanksgiving, we gave away hundreds of turkeys to the needy.

A Chicago alderman approached us, and we got involved in community services. Our members showed up to march against human trafficking and other crimes. All of this brought attention to the church and let people know that it was alive again.

At first, I didn't know any of the local pastors, except one Indian pastor whose father was a good friend of mine. I told him I wanted to get to know the other pastors in the city, with the goal of forming a ministerial fellowship. He said, "It will never work. We tried it before, but it never progressed."

I said, "Well, why don't you and I meet once a week and start praying together, and then we can invite other pastors?"

We started and invited others, and it grew. During Thanksgiving week of 1997, we had a gathering at the UIC (University of Chicago) Pavilion (now renamed the Credit Union 1 Arena) for prayer for the nation, and nearly ten thousand people from many different churches attended. We did that twice, and that brought us more recognition in the city.

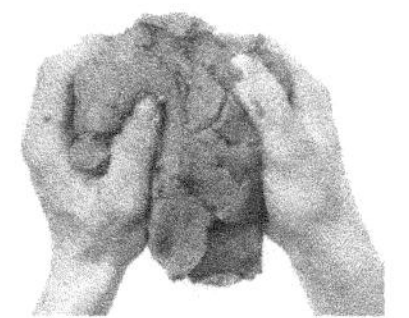

65

ANOTHER OF THE ISSUES THAT TROUBLED ME GREATLY WHEN I FIRST became pastor of Faith Tabernacle was my discovery of the fact that the church had made commitments to support missionaries, seven or eight full-time missionaries, and then, when hard times came, had reneged on these commitments. When I arrived there, missionary support had not been paid for the past four years. I was furious. No wonder the church couldn't pay its bills!

I was still steaming when I confronted the members of the board. I said, "This makes you all liars and cheaters. You are fulfilling this and that, but you have robbed these people and put them in a very difficult situation. They were depending on the support you promised."

The secretary of the church spoke up and said, "But we just couldn't afford it."

I said, "We cannot afford *not* to send it. Now that the church has money, I want us to send the promised support and also pay these missionaries back what the church owes them. If you want the church to be blessed, we have to do this. And I don't want any argument."

I later said to my secretary, "Give me the names, addresses, and phone number of all those missionaries." I sent them letters, saying, "If you are still in the mission field, let me know and how to send you the promised support." I apologized for the negligence of the church in not sending what they had promised. "Now that I am the pastor, I would like to make good on the church's commitments."

My letter continued, "As long as you are in the mission field, we will continue to support you. But even if you are no longer in the mission field, we want to pay you back what the church owes you." They all responded, and we paid them back everything in arrears. When we did that, the Lord honored it and brought more blessings to the church. Many of those missionaries later came and visited the church, and it was a powerful testimony.

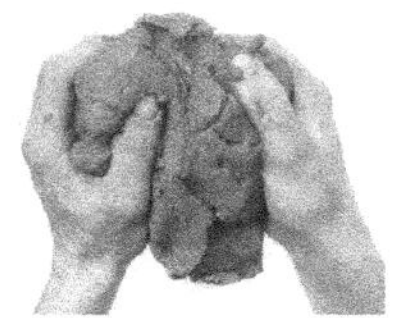

66

Now, we began to get involved again with mission programs around the world. We started supporting other missionaries, and very early on, I began making mission trips myself and taking along members of the church. We went to Nigeria, Ghana, and Liberia in West Africa, to Thailand, to Belize in Central America, to China, Vietnam, and India. I also took a group to Israel. All of this created a wonderful excitement in the church, causing others to join with our vision and loosing finances for the purposes of God's Kingdom.

After we had totally paid off that heavy debt the church had been operating under, we were able to have a greater outreach, not only within our own community, but also around the world. We established a church in Hong Kong, where we found a great open door. Suddenly, the people of the church got very excited.

Some who had been holding back their tithes started giving again. One lady, an elderly nurse, living alone, brought a check for more than $12,000. She said, "I had not given my tithes for three years because I didn't trust the leadership." Now giving continued to climb, and the church was flourishing.

I made a trip to China and brought some members with me. I went to speak in New Zealand, and the mission that had invited me booked me into other New Zealand churches.

Then this excitement affected my own family. In 1999, Steve and Joy and their two children felt called to become missionaries to the Philippines, and Faith Tabernacle sent them and supported them. They were based in Cebu, but Steve traveled all over Asia. They spent more time in Indonesia and Malaysia than they did in the Philippines.

My son David worked in Manila for a while, then came to work with me in the church in Chicago. Leah returned to the Philippines to finish her studies and worked with the church there. She had been there many years and planned to stay longer. I asked her to move back and work with me in Chicago, but she reminded me that I always taught them to seek the will of God for their lives. What could I say?

The work in the Philippines continued to prosper. Since I had been in Chicago, the school in Manila had to expand. More playground area had to be built. An open area was covered and divided into more classrooms to accommodate additional students. Even with this, the school was actively seeking to purchase a nearby property on which to expand. But property values had continued to soar. An available lot of two thousand square meters now cost forty million pesos.

The church continued to do well, and the brothers there had been going out to minister in Vietnam, Thailand, Bangladesh, and Korea. Select students from the school had begun doing missionary work. The choir traveled to minister in churches in Korea, Hong Kong, and China. How good the Lord is!

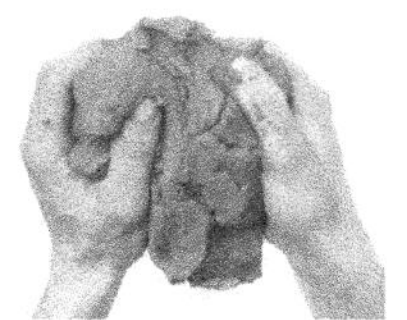

67

Our outreach continued in other ways. One of the Filipino families from our church in Manila moved to Winnipeg, Canada. They missed the kind of "fired-up" services we had shared in Manila and told me they wanted to start a church in Winnipeg. "Why don't you begin with a Bible study in your home," I suggested, and see what God will do.

After I moved to Chicago, I went to Winnipeg to visit them to help them structure the study, then we sent them materials to use, and I visited them as I was able. On one of my visits, I noticed that they were really growing. I suggested that they take turns ministering and start some serious public meetings, and I began to look around for a site where such meetings could be held.

My first thought was to check with local churches to see if they would allow us to use their building some afternoons. I called a Pentecostal church and told them who I was and why I was calling. "Why not come and meet us, and we can discuss it?" was the answer.

As it turned out, the pastor of the church had been feeling a burden for the many Filipinos moving into the community. "This would be a wonderful thing, if you can reach out to this community," he said. "I'll present it to the board, and I don't expect there will be any problem."

The rent was to be Canadian $100 a week, but we were already receiving offerings in our Bible study, so the money was available.

The board approved our use of the building, and I went back to organize the church. I asked the pastor of the other church if he would be willing to sit in on some of the services, and even preach to the people. He agreed and spoke for them on many Sundays when they did not have another speaker scheduled.

Now the group had Sunday school, Bible study and prayer meetings. They had begun with just a few, but by 1998, they had fifty people in attendance already.

After only a few months, the pastor of the church we were renting said to me, "Brother Ray, we are moving from this place. We have bought a larger property, and we are in the process of remodeling it. So, this property will soon be for sale. But we will not sell it to anybody else but your people."

"That's wonderful," I said, "but we can't afford it."

"Well," he answered, "in that case, let me talk to the board and see what we can do." In the end, the Assembly of God of Canada agreed to hold the mortgage on the building, and we made monthly payments to them.

When the local congregation moved into their new building in December of 1999, the Filipino service moved to Sunday morning. Something else happened at about the same time.

As far back as 1997, we had been praying for a proper pastor for the church. I had recommended a man I knew in the Philippines. The church petitioned for him to receive a visa, and it took him two years to work out his papers. In December of 1999, he arrived. Under his leadership the church prospered. They not only bought the church; they also bought the parsonage next to it. Now, they are running more than three hundred in their services.

In 2002, the pastor called to say that he wanted me to come and help them look for a larger place. I told him the steps to take and suggested that they look for a suitable location themselves. They were out of Sunday school space, parking was a problem, and they had outgrown the sanctuary — all wonderful problems to have.

Later on, the man who was the key person in getting all of that started in Winnipeg moved to Memphis, Tennessee. There he met some Filipinos and suggested that they start a Bible study together. He called me to say that they had fifteen of them already meeting regularly and that I needed to come and organize the church. That group is praying for a pastor, and I have someone in mind whom I think we could bring over.

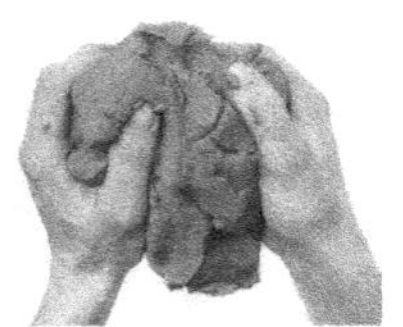

68

I was at Faith Tabernacle for almost seven years, and during that time God blessed and prospered us. But early on, I had told the congregation that I was only there on assignment. When the Lord spoke to my heart that it was time to move on, they would have no hold over me. When that time came, it was not difficult for me. It was easy.

What was next for me? The Lord did not release me to leave Chicago. He told me, "Open another ministry." And that's what I intended to do.

On Father's Day in 2002, I resigned from Faith Tabernacle, and one of the associate pastors took over. My final Sunday was to be the last Sunday in July. I then waited two months before starting the new work.

Some had advised me to announce to the Faith Tabernacle congregation what I intended to do, but I couldn't do that. I didn't want to split the church. Nobody knew what I was doing except the board members. I had told them, "I'm not leaving the city because God has another assignment for me here."

I started the new work quietly. There were others who followed me, twelve of us in all, and we first began praying to know the will of God. We didn't announce anything until we were ready to launch. After three months, I felt that it was time to start anew. The Lord had said to me, "Go into the Lincolnwood area." This was quite far from Faith Tabernacle.

We rented a room in the Holiday Inn there in Lincolnwood. I had spoken to the owners, and they gave us a very good price.

We rented the space on Sundays and Wednesdays, and that was where we started.

That was in July of 2002, and for the first Sunday service, we had just a handful of people. On the second Sunday, there were a lot more. Those who had come had called friends who were not involved in any church, and they came too. We had nearly 180 that day in attendance.

We soon outgrew the hotel and moved to the auditorium of Lake View High School on West Irving Park Road. It seated 1,200, and we had a lot of activities there. We had campmeetings there. We had an Easter production that drew more than 1,500. We did the performance the Saturday evening before Easter and again on Easter Sunday. The place was packed. What a powerful presentation!

Joy was running the musical department of the church and had a cast of 100 telling the story of Jesus and His ministry. It culminated with the crucifixion and the resurrection. That production brought more people into the church.

We had services there for a long time, and then decided it was time for us to start looking for a property to buy. On Wednesday night, when the Spirit of God was moving or during our campmeetings, we had to abort the services because we had to be out by 9:00 pm. Sometimes, it was awkward to stop when the Spirit of God was still moving.

We found a warehouse for sale, but the city would not change the zoning codes to allow a church to use it. We fought with City Hall and with the Zoning Commission to change the zoning.

We prayed, and then we hired a Christian lawyer. She went to quite a few hearings, but after six or seven months, there was still no ruling. The owner was a Jewish man. At this point, we made him a proposal. We wanted to buy the place, but only under the condition that the zoning would be changed to allow church use. He signed the contract, and we moved in (hoping to save our rent money) even before there was a ruling on the zoning change. It was a step of faith.

In time, the zoning was changed, and we remodeled the place. That was quite a job remodeling such an old building, but God helped us, and the church continued to grow. The Assemblies of God helped us to secure financing through the Church Extension Plan, loaning us the money to buy the property and also for the remodeling.

We soon started a radio program and started doing mission work. I made quite a few trips to the Philippines, taking many from the church. We made trips to Belize, to Nigeria, and to India as well.

In 2005, we started a ministry in Honduras called Harvest Christian Center. It was a church and a Christian school. One of the pastors we had trained in the Philippines learned to speak Spanish, and God called him to pastor that work.

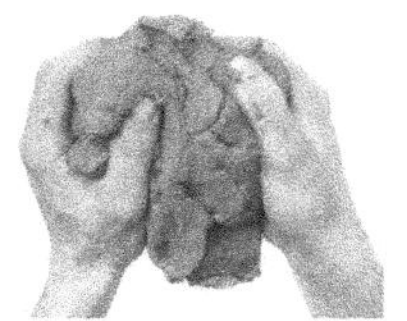

69

In June of 2010, while I was on a plane from Chicago to Minneapolis to get a connecting flight to the Philippines, my son kept calling me. Because I was in flight, his calls went unanswered. It was only when I landed that I got his messages. I called him back, and he told me that the church there in Metro Manila had caught fire.

In that moment, it seemed to me like the whole world had collapsed. I felt as if the heavens had dropped over me, and I was buried alive. I couldn't speak for a moment. When I had regained my composure, I asked, "Well, did it burn the whole building?" He said he couldn't tell yet how much actual damage had been done.

When I arrived in the Philippines, my children picked me up from the airport, and I went directly to the church. The building was still smoldering, although the fire had been put out. I stood and wept. Then the Lord spoke to me. He said, "A building can be burned, but the soul will never be destroyed."

In the coming days, we were better able to assess the damages. All of the sound equipment in the sanctuary, valued at nearly $150,000, had been destroyed. Other equipment, valued at $50,000, was also destroyed. The chairs and other furnishings were beyond saving. All that remained were walls and ceiling. Although the fire had been contained in the sanctuary, other parts of the building had been severely damaged from the water the firemen used to keep the fire from spreading. All of our computers and musical instruments were destroyed, and our offices and classrooms were severely damaged. The damage was so great that the insurance would not nearly cover it. Because we had a good record, we were able to borrow from the bank enough to begin the reconstruction.

We shut down the school for two weeks to clean up all the debris and to make the classrooms presentable and healthy enough for the students to return. We would have to replace all of the equipment.

We totally remodeled the sanctuary and repaired the damage in the classrooms and the lab. We bought all new sound equipment and all new instruments for the lab.

The library had also been damaged, and we had to throw away all of the books we had accumulated and start over. During the first service after the fire, the Lord spoke to me in prophecy. He said, "Out of the ashes I will gather the remnants, and out of the remnant, I will raise a nation, and out of the nation I will build a great and mighty army." That now became our motto, as the church and the school, by the grace of God, continued to operate.

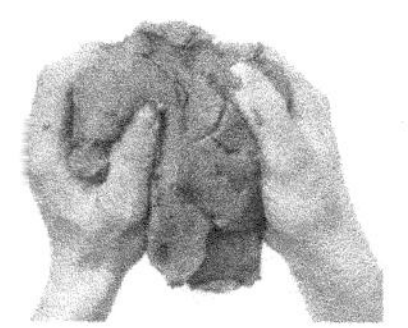

70

In 2012, the Lord began to speak to my heart to go back to the Philippines. Here, again, I was going back to the country I was from. It may have seemed to others that I was going back and forth, but I knew when it was the Lord's will. I had never hesitated to obey and follow Him. I had proven through the years that wherever God guides He provides. I had been going back and forth between 2009 and 2012, and now I resigned the church in 2014 and moved to the Philippines permanently.

I had a crisis on my hands. The church I had founded in our country needed revived. The church needed rebuilding and has since started flourishing again. We are now putting up new church buildings in the provinces. We have had land donated and are in the middle of a building project in the province of Sorsogon. The construction is in progress, and we are believing God to provide the funds to finish it.

My base is now the Philippines, and I come once or twice a year to the United States to visit and to raise funds for the ministry. I also spend two to three months a year in Europe, primarily in Italy and Spain, speaking in different churches and also in conferences. I have a few churches that I am mentoring in Italy. I thank God for a ministry that is worldwide.

We took our senior high students, before they graduated, on a missions trip outside of the Philippines. We went to Hong Kong and Singapore, and we're now getting ready to go to Cambodia. The students raised their own money to go on this mission trip, and some of them have been called to the ministry and have gone on to college, with the goal of eventually becoming pastors. We thank God for this outreach.

The school is doing great, and we are improving the building. There are many things that need fixed. We need to upgrade the building because it's rather old now and needs some work on the roof and the walls. But God is good, and we are excited about what He has for us in the future.

71

AMAZINGLY, DURING THE PANDEMIC, WE BUILT THREE CHURCHES IN the Philippines. I still don't know how we did it or where the money came from. When the lands were donated to us, I said to the leadership of the church, "The land has been donated, and so we need to build." I was able to rally the people, and we started building.

I traveled to the United States to raise money, but it was not enough. Still, we finished all three churches during the pandemic, and it was a testimony to what God can do. The Filipino economy had collapsed, and many churches had closed their doors. Some of our people who were businessmen had lost their businesses, and others were laid off from their jobs. Still, God provided, this time from different sources.

These church buildings were finished without incurring any debt. God's economy doesn't experience inflation or recession. We can trust in and depend on His promises. He is faithful, no matter what may come our way. In every situation, in every condition, His Word always prevails.

We are currently looking for a property for one of our growing churches, this one in Calamba, Laguna. The congregation has outgrown their rented facilities and want to have their own building. So we are raising funds for that. We know that the Lord will provide. It is yet another step of faith.

Because of what we have experienced in the past, I am much bolder now and more confident than ever. I have a record of God's faithfulness and commitment to His promises.

God had spoken to me many years ago during the construction of our building in San Juan, that money was not the problem. I needed to concentrate on faith and obedience. When we obey the Lord and we trust Him, He will prove to us that He is faithful and His Word will never fail. He would never lie to us, His children. I'm rejoicing in the Lord and He is continuing to bless.

My son David resigned from his job here in the U.S. and moved to the Philippines to help us in the ministry. There he found his wife. She is now the principal of our school, and I'm grooming David to take over the ministry when I'm gone. It will continue.

We are now pioneering a new church in the city of Cubao, Quezon City, and David is pastoring that work. For now, we have a rented space in the Gateway Mall, but the people are hopeful that one day they will have their own permanent building for worship. Because that work is so young, we help to support them financially.

I am now busier than ever, raising up leaders and mentoring pastors, conducting family conferences, campmeetings, and leadership seminars. I am also traveling all over the Philippines and other parts of Asia, and around the world. In recent years, I have made quite a few visits to Nigeria, West Africa, and they are inviting me again. This coming September, I will be in Norway.

To aid all of our activities for the Lord, I was led to register in the city of Chicago our ministry covering. It is called Global Evangelistic Ministries. Our ministry in the Philippines is now under that covering, and promoting the mission is now the main thrust of my ministry.

As a grandfather, I am excited about the next generations, and we have many young people who are on fire for the Lord, and we're working with them. They have a great future. I am confident that what we have started, they will finish with the Lord's help.

The Lord spoke to me one day that the glory of the latter house will be greater than the former. In our upcoming conference this year (2024), our emphasis will be on church planting. Our vision is that in the next five years we will plant ten NEW churches. After the conference, we will celebrate our anniversary of the ministry in the Philippines. So I'm very excited for what the future holds for us. God's Word tells us:

No eye has seen, no ear has heard,
and no mind has imagined
what God has prepared
for those who love him. 1 Corinthians 2:9, NLT

I believe it!

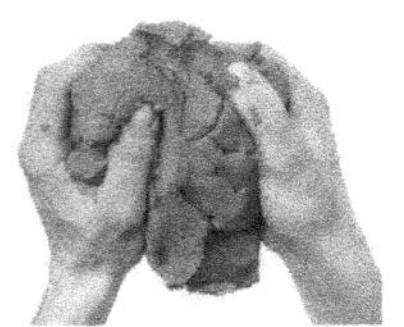

72

I AM NOW NEARING EIGHTY, BUT I KNOW THAT GOD HAS MORE GREAT things in store for me, more wonderful things that He will do, more than I have seen in the past eighty years. I am grateful to the Lord that, in spite of who I am, He picked me up and gave me the opportunity to experience what He can do through a humble instrument submitted to Him and cooperating with Him. Thank God. This is my story.

Author Contact Page

You may contact Bishop Ray Llarena directly at:

Global Evangelistic Ministries
9039 Lakeshore Dr.
Pleasant Prairie, WI 53158

Email: bishopray1@yahoo.com

www.ingramcontent.com/pod-product-compliance
Lightning Source LLC
Chambersburg PA
CBHW021220090426
42740CB00006B/306

* 9 7 8 1 5 8 1 5 8 2 0 9 3 *